The author was born in 1947 and has lived all of her life in Lincolnshire. She has worked in a variety of jobs, including retailing and social services. Having a heart for the marginalised, she has been on many overseas aid missions. During her forties, Joy experienced a call from God to train for ministry in the church. Gaining a B.A. in theology and pastoral studies from Theological College, she went on to train and work as a prison chaplain at HM Prison Lincoln. Having being involved in the lives of many prisoners and staff, this book captures the day-to-day life of prison and highlights the pain and difficulties together with humour felt by many in the service. After retirement, Joy continues to serve in the church and enjoys the more leisurely pursuits of walking and exploring castles and historical houses.

This book is dedicated to the memory of the late Reverend Canon Alan Richard Duce. (1941–2006)

Joy Osborne

AN INSIDE JOB

THE LIFE OF A PRISON CHAPLAIN

AUSTIN MACAULEY PUBLISHERS™

LONDON • CAMBRIDGE • NEW YORK • SHARJAH

A CIP catalogue record for this title is available from the British Library.

ISBN 9781528998529 (Paperback)
ISBN 9781528998536 (ePub e-book)

www.austinmacauley.com

First Published 2021
Austin Macauley Publishers Ltd ®
1 Canada Square,
Canary Wharf,
London,
E14 5AA
+44 (0)20 7038 8212
+44 (0)20 3515 0352

In writing this book, I pay tribute to all who work in the prison service, especially colleagues at HM Prison Lincoln, with whom I shared the day-to-day life of the prison.

The chaplaincy team and prison visitors became close friends and I commend them for their tireless ministry.

I am grateful to the Church of the Nazarene for its support in recommending and ordaining me for the role of prison chaplain and to district superintendents, Reverend Clive Burrows and Reverend David Montgomery, for their guidance and visits to the prison.

My thanks go to Chris and the local prison fellowship group for their faithfulness in ministry in support of prisoners and prison chaplains.

Appreciation is given to friend and typist, Jayne, for her assistance; to Velma for secretarial help and to author, Lucy Wood, for proof reading this book.

Last but not the least, to my husband, Eric, whose love and support is constant; and to God for nudging me forward to new pastures and an exciting and demanding ministry.

Information and statistics are accurate for the time I worked in the prison service. However, things change very frequently. Practices and systems that were in place then may have changed or been updated. Some names have been changed to respect confidentiality.

Although over 80,000 men and women are housed in British prisons, the vast majority of the public have little or no idea what life behind the prison gate is like.

Within those walls are people from all walks of life. Some are a danger to themselves or to others. The vast majority serve their sentence quietly as they endure the tedium and monotony of prison life.

The work of a prison chaplain is complex and demanding. Many prisoners simply need someone to listen to them as they attempt to make sense of their disrupted lives. Others need to be reinforced by hearing a message of hope; a message that says whatever crime has been committed, forgiveness is possible. Here a good chaplain will be at hand with compassionate care and support.

Joy Osborne has written simply and directly about her experience of working with some of the most vulnerable people in society. Her book will help increase the understanding of what life is like for many prisoners and their families.

– Terry Waite CBE

This brief book is full of stories and insights about prison chaplaincy. Joy's compassionate spirit shines through, as well as the sense that the people she has helped care for over the years are precious and unfinished – and that, in encounters with them, God reveals something of how brokenness can be met with a loving presence and kind heart. There is no doubt that readers will be enriched and brought to a point on how God reveals mercy in institutions that are sometimes stretched thin. Chaplaincy is a gift that helps knit people together again – and weeps at those times where that doesn't happen. The impression I get is of a strong, gentle woman whose calling is fulfilled by steady presence in hard places.

– Reverend Dr Deirdre Brower Latz
Principal,
Nazarene Theological College, Manchester

Table of Contents

Joy Osborne's book is more than a window on the role of a prison chaplain. It is an intimate account of standing alongside people in the extremes of life. Grief, death, bereavement, frustrations, sadness, and even joy are all present within this reflection on what is an all-consuming ministry. It is filled with 'story', a testimony to an often unseen service. Few will have had the privilege and the burden of the work that Joy has undertaken, but all who have will recognise the pressures associated with keeping people secure and those sacramental moments when a new awakening occurs in the lives of the perplexed. And for those who have never visited a prison I would commend it as a significant contribution to understanding a much overlooked part of our world today. It is inspiring.

– The Reverend Bruce Thompson
Chair Lincolnshire Methodist District

Foreword

I have known Joy for many years and have been privileged to have had a small part in her ministry journey. This has included being a part of the selection process for ministry candidates in her denomination, serving for a number of years as her District Superintendent and as a fellow Pastor and colleague, but most of all, as just another servant of Christ and His Kingdom, fulfilling His call to service.

It was a special delight to participate in her Induction Service at Lincoln Prison in July 2002 and, some 16 months later, visit the prison and spend time with Joy. She showed me around various departments and I observed her interaction with prisoners and staff, just over a year after the prison riot of 2002.

Before this, my knowledge and experience of prison life was limited to visiting inmates at HM Prison Wakefield on a few occasions and HM Prison Manchester (or Strangeways, as those of us brought up in the locality always called it).

Though visiting as an ordained minister, my wife and I joined the long queue of visitors outside Strangeways on a cold and damp Manchester morning. Families flowed through the gate for security check before being ushered into a large visiting room where there was little privacy and heavy surveillance. This was before the infamous riots at the prison. The chaplain, Noel Proctor, proved helpful to us in future visits. We learned how essential it is to remember to pray, especially for the guys we visited during the evening hours of 'lockdown', when they were confined to the loneliness and isolation of their cell.

During my years of missionary service, I took services in Bissau Prison, Mt Hagen, Papua New Guinea, and later participated in services in Chisinau Prison, Moldova. After speaking with inmates in Chisinau who were about to be released, I left the clothes I took with me (a month's worth), for they had so little to face freedom with. It was there I learned that not every story has a positive outcome. One of the released prisoners who attended the services which my Moldovan friends conducted so faithfully went on to murder a woman who had given him a great deal of support and assistance.

My experience was that of the outside observer, catching brief and incomplete snapshots of prison life and ministry. My time spent with Joy and several conversations with her over the years gave me more of a window to flesh out these images. Reading her book, written in such straightforward, unembroidered language, gives a more complete picture of life for inmates, officers and the day-to-day work of prison chaplains.

The book is interesting, revealing and very moving. I recommend it to all those who desire to understand prison life and ministry better but also to those who, to this point, have never considered the needs and opportunities that are part of the life of significantly large numbers of our population, to have any relevance for them.

Joy is an unassuming Christian who allowed Christ to open doors to ministry and so was led into ministries she never could have imagined. She learned to trust Christ in supporting her through some of the most difficult years of HM Lincoln Prison's recent history. This book reminds us powerfully that ministry is all about people.

The beautiful Biblical word 'redemption' reminds us all that in Christ there is provision for our own emancipation and deliverance from everything that imprisons or enslaves us. Joy's book is also a powerful reminder that God's call to the 'ministry of reconciliation' often comes to those who seem to be—in the eyes of many and indeed of themselves —totally unsuited and unprepared for such a calling (1 Corinthians 1:26-31). Read this with an open mind and heart to hear what God might be saying to you.

– Reverend Clive Burrows M.A. PGCE
Retired Pastor, Missionary, Theological Lecturer, Cross Cultural Missions Specialist and District Superintendent, Church of the Nazarene.

Chapter One
The Beginnings

It was never my intention to stun someone into silence but this was usually the response when asked the question, "What is your job"? To most people, the work of a prison chaplain is unknown, something to which they cannot relate to. Why should they? Fortunately for a large part of the population, they have never entered the world of the unknown. Life behind bars! However, as they start to consider that they are looking at and speaking to someone who has knowledge of life on the inside; the conversation goes along an interesting path.

To give an honest and accurate answer to the question, "How did I become involved in prison ministry?" I must go back many years to when I first became a Christian. Having being brought up as a child in the Christian faith, it was easy to consider that I already was a Christian! It wasn't until a series of life events led me to attend an evangelistic crusade in my hometown that I was faced with the question, "Do you know Jesus Christ personally as Lord and Saviour?" The preacher giving out this appeal spoke with such conviction that I felt I ought to give the question some serious thought. The invitation to publicly respond, move out my seat and go to front of the hall took faith—an enormous amount of faith— but I was convinced that God was speaking directly to me. It was a decision that I have never regretted. Of course, life has not always been a bed of roses, but this was the start a new life, a journey into the future with a new family called church, with Jesus at the centre.

As a stranger, I was welcomed in to the church and encouraged to exercise my natural gifts of care and compassion that my parents had instilled in me as a child.

Early in the 1990s, I was invited by my church to join with them in taking aid to Romania. This was the first of many trips to that country following the revolution and overthrowing of the country's president, Nicolae Ceausescu. To see the many poor people living in squalor with next to nothing to exist on, deprived of the bare necessities of life, was heart breaking. Equally so, were the rows and rows of orphans who filled the orphanages to the point that they were overflowing. There was too little in the way of medicine, baby clothes, sheets, blankets, food and cleaning materials. In fact, there was despair and hopelessness, their eyes dull with lack of stimulation and no support. In the midst of such chaos, we were welcomed with open arms. The scripture from Proverbs 22:9 comes to mind:

"He who has a generous eye will be blessed. For he gives of his bread to the poor." (NKJV).

I thank God every day for the blessings He gives me.

Was this the beginning, a taste of what ministry to the marginalised means? But surely God was not sending me overseas to work! However, He had something in mind—a plan for my life of ministry which began with study at Nazarene Theological College, Manchester. I had no specific thoughts of becoming a church minister, so what could it be? The scripture says in Jeremiah 29:11: "For I know the plans I have for you," declares the Lord, "plans to prosper you and not to harm you, plans to give you a hope and a future" (NIV). With this in mind I was confident of one thing. God was in control!

It was in the autumn of 1995 and the church was preparing to celebrate harvest festival. Our minister at the time, the late Reverend Fred Grossmith, an accomplished musician, suggested we might invite Reverend David Casswell and his band Poetic Justice. David was chaplain at the Wolds Prison, in the county that was then known as North Humberside. He composed all the songs that the six-piece band played. Their intention was to communicate the despair, pain and Christian hope of many in prison. This they did very effectively.

Until this point, I had never given prison any thought. I had not considered the work of a prison chaplain and certainly not the life of a prisoner. I and my family were in the fortunate position of never having been incarcerated. Why would I want to concern myself with prison now?

Following this encounter of what life is like for the prisoner, their family and loved ones, a series of coincidences happened. I prefer to call them 'God-incidences', as nothing happens by chance for the believer in Jesus Christ.

I discovered that there had been an active Prison Fellowship (PF) group some years ago in my home area. It had disbanded. How sad, I thought, as I reflected on Revd. Casswell and what life must be like for him, helping many prisoners and being involved in a wide variety of situations.

I felt that God was saying to me: "There is something you can do. What about PF?" I did some research into the organisation, its aims and purpose with the help of my friend Chris, who also had a heart for prison ministry. God put across our path some former members of the group, who were delighted to think that the local group may be re-established.

The history of PF began in the USA in the 1970s. It was at the height of the Watergate affair when Chuck Colson, who was special counsel to President Richard Nixon, committed his life to Christ. Shortly afterwards, he was given a seven-month prison sentence for his part in the Watergate conspiracy. His time spent in prison showed him the importance of a Christian witness in prisons. On the basis of his experiences, he founded PF and it became a worldwide organisation, called Prison Fellowship International. At about the same time in England, Sylvia Mary Alison believed God was calling her to develop Christian ministry in our prisons but was not clear about the way forward. Once she heard of PF, she believed this was the answer to her prayers and so in 1979, Prison Fellowship England and Wales was founded. It has 2,500 volunteers and aims to have a prayer group supporting all of our 120 prisons. Assisting in chapel services and running PF programmes are just a small part of what the group offer to our prisons and chaplains.

Word spread that the local PF Group had re-formed. Like-minded people, including Christians from various churches around the area, asked to join. I was asked if I would become their PF leader, a role which I threw myself into wholeheartedly.

To become an accredited volunteer of PF, it was expected that the members would complete a series of exercises (core competencies) from the work book 'Equipping the Saints'. Upon completion of the ten units, a certificate of accreditation was awarded from PF. I enjoyed working with other Christians from a wide variety of churches. As PF's Christian base is founded upon the Nicene Creed, it was easy to find common ground. We met on a regular basis and prayed to God as to where, what and how we could become effective in supporting our prisons and former offenders. There is nothing like experience to gain a feel of the work that you have committed to. I learned early on that I was entering a delicate ministry. Life for the prisoner and their family is often raw and tensions are felt either side of the fence.

"Can you give some support to a wife while her husband is in HMP Whatton?" asked the person on the other end of the phone from a PF group in the Nottingham area. It seemed like a reasonable request, so I went to the house in an area of the town quite unfamiliar to me to meet Jane and her family. There was one child who was unaware of his father's whereabouts. There was an atmosphere of unease and the conversation was strained as I enquired about the family's welfare. Jane said she felt isolated. The fact that her husband's offence was of a sexual nature – which he categorically denied having committed, made it more difficult to deal with. Although she could get to the prison to visit, it was a difficult journey, as I was a driver, and available, it seemed the natural thing to offer her a lift. She gladly accepted, explaining she was waiting for her husband to send a visiting order and that it would take a few weeks.

As Jane didn't seem to want any further help, I left the house.

My life quickly filled up with other things and apart from occasionally remembering the family in prayer, thoughts of travelling to Whatton had long gone from my mind, until one day, the phone rang. "This is Jane; can you take me to the prison tomorrow?" For a moment I was stunned. There was no "How are you, do you remember me?" but only an expectancy that I would do as requested. Unfortunately, I was unavailable: I had an urgent appointment that couldn't be cancelled. The tone of her voice changed. I could sense the anger and disappointment as she reminded me of my promise. Of course she was upset! It's only now, as I look back, that I see how foolish I had been in the choice of words I used; perhaps giving the impression I was available at short notice. My apology didn't seem adequate; was she being unreasonable and I insensitive?

Now, after eleven years as prison chaplain, I would not make the same mistake again. The lesson was learned at someone else's expense. If I had been in Jane's shoes, I would probably have felt the same. How lonely she must have felt. Perhaps she too was used to rejection.

By now, the group was keen to get some practical experience. This we did at HMP Everthorpe (a male category C prison) and Morton Hall (at the time a male category D prison) and Lincoln (category B), where we were welcomed by the chaplain, Reverend Canon Alan Duce, at the Sunday services. The training we had received from PF, together with our church ministry gifts of preaching, singing and reading from the scriptures, were now being put into practice. We took the good news of the gospel to the prisoners and reflected on the words of Jesus, from Matthew 25:34–36: "Then the king will say to those on His right hand, come you blessed of my Father, inherit the kingdom prepared for you from the foundation of the world: for I was hungry and you gave Me food: I was thirsty and you gave Me a drink: I was a stranger and you took Me in; I was naked and you clothed Me, I was sick and you visited Me, I was in prison and you came to Me." NKJV.

The reality of these words was coming true, not only for me but for each member of the group. God's love was being taken inside, to a world that was as yet unknown to us.

Prison Fellowship https;/prisonfellowship.org.uk

Chapter Two
Open Doors

The three prisons we initially visited were in varying categories and, as such, were all different in their approach and security measures.

Our first introduction to Everthorpe prison, which was modernised in 1991 and later joined with The Wolds to form one prison, The Humber was at a harvest festival service. We received a warm welcome from the chaplain and prisoners, who took an active part in the proceedings. They had many natural talents and I was particularly impressed by their drama presentations. There was plenty of opportunity for conversation with the prisoners over refreshments after the service, too. The chapel was a modern design with study rooms and quiet spaces. Although the prison was guarded by high walls and gates, it seemed to have a relaxed atmosphere. However, the prison rules for visitors were never far from our minds: Nothing in and nothing out.

Some fifty miles away was Morton Hall. Previously an RAF base, it was established as an open prison in 1985 for male prisoners. Today it is an Immigration Removal Centre for male detainees, and was a sharp contrast to Everthorpe. There were no high walls and few restrictions. It almost seemed as though prisoners could come and go as they pleased and perhaps some of them did! However, the prison was off the beaten track so I wouldn't think they would get far very easily. But there's always a way for those who are determined!

Like Everthorpe, the chapel was modern, light and airy. We attended a traditional Sunday service led by the lady chaplain and afterwards, we sat in a circle for refreshments and discussions. This seemed even more relaxed than the previous prison; if the detainees hadn't been wearing prison clothes, one would never have known they were prisoners at all. They would have fitted in quite nicely around the dining table at home!

What had been my perception of a prisoner? What did he look like and say, how did he act? I didn't know then, but I was going to gain an insight over the coming years. It made me realise that we are all human beings and I believed these men were no different from anyone else. Everyone had a personal story to tell of how they had come to be inside.

Ten miles from Morton Hall lay HMP Lincoln. This was entirely different. A huge perimeter wall surrounded the prison. As usual our security checks were carried out and we were taken through several locked gates to the chapel.

The prison opened as a local jail in 1872. It serves the courts of Lincolnshire, Nottinghamshire and Humberside. Inside are men who have committed a range of crimes, including sex offences, murder, drug-related burglary and motoring offences to name but a few. Some are on remand; some are serving life sentences and others indeterminate sentences for public protection.

Although the prison has a rolling programme of refurbishment, three of the four main residential units are of its original Victorian design, as is the chapel. Modern fire regulations state it cannot hold more than one hundred people but it was designed to hold many.

The chaplain, the late Reverend Canon Alan Duce, welcomed us into the huge chapel and gave instructions as to how the service would progress. I was grateful that we also had members of the local PF group from Lincoln to give support and guidance. "Where are the prisoners?" I asked Alan. "They will come through at the top gate with the prison officers", he replied.

It seemed a long time but eventually they appeared in the chapel: young, old and in-between, chattering, laughing, quiet, sullen, hopeful, despondent and expectant. Eventually the service began. I discovered it is the chaplain's job to keep his congregation in order if needed, unless, of course, a disturbance breaks out. Then, the officers who are present throughout services will intervene.

Most of my group were to take part with reading and singing and I giving the sermon, which was considerably shorter than in church as we were on a tight time schedule. The chapel service was part of the day's activities and, as such, had to fit in with the regime of the prison.

I started to feel nervous as time went on. The chaplain had asked one of my readers to speak up, and I wondered how I would get on. The chapel was a large and spacious place, going up in layers to the double gates at the back. Some of the prisoners sat up there, so I could see that my voice would need to carry a long way if it was going to have any impact.

My turn came to deliver the sermon. All eyes were on me. There was a deadly hush. I remember thinking: "If there is any noise, I shall be put off and grind to a halt!" But there wasn't. Not a soul moved. Not a word spoken. They looked transfixed as I pressed on and preached what I thought was a suitable sermon from one of the gospels. I came to the end and was about to sit down when cheering and clapping erupted from the men. I looked at them, astonished, and felt myself going as red as a beetroot. Nothing ever happened to me like this before. It certainly would not in church back home. The chaplain quickly took charge and things moved on.

At the end of the service, we chatted with as many prisoners as time would allow. They thanked us for coming and were keen to take the Christian literature we handed out.

As we talked with the chaplain and the more experienced local PF volunteers, some interesting feedback and encouragement was given. "Well Joy," said Stephen. "I think you and the group did very well for the first time but the sermon you preached was so in depth theologically that it went over their heads!"

I was grateful for his comments. As I watched the crowd of prisoners intently looking at me, it never occurred that possibly they hadn't understood a word I was saying! However, I was to learn that a prison congregation is made up of men in different situations. There are some who cannot read and have difficulty in singing from a hymn book. There are others who just want to get out of their cells for an hour and meet up with mates from other wings. And there are men who want to be there because they are from a church background or want to discover the Christian faith. Some did want to take part in the service, read the scriptures and play the piano or organ. In the seemingly mixed jumble of prisoners, there was a large amount of talent and even those who appeared to be indifferent could be encouraged to find their place. Whatever his background or crime—and remember, some were still on remand in this jail—he was still a human being created in the image of God. Whatever had brought the prisoner into the chapel that day, I prayed that he made a connection with God and would return the following Sunday. Little did I know then that I would be seeing some of them for many years to come!

The chaplain was keen to welcome us on a regular basis so we worked out a rota for the coming months. As time went on, it became apparent that the group could not sustain supporting all three prisons by our presence at Sunday services. Following prayer and deliberation, we decided to channel our energies into HMP Lincoln. The group had grown to about fourteen members who met monthly for prayer and information. They were a committed bunch and always eager to engage in various avenues of service within PF relating to prisoners and their families, as well as ex-offenders. They were keen to meet other PF members across the area, and joined in training days and other events for mutual support. I was privileged to be their leader.

My studies at Nazarene College continued. Each year, I met with the Board of Ministry to assess my academic and practical progress. I was no nearer hearing that call from God to a specific ministry location… or was I?

Each time we visited the jail, my heart leapt. Going into the unknown was not a frightening experience. Although I was security conscious and aware of prison rules regarding confidentiality and personal information, I never let this get in the way of having meaningful conversations with the prisoners. I was often asked: "How do the prisoners treat you? Are they respectful?" To which I could honestly answer: "Very well, and yes."

Having now had a taste of prison ministry, I was keen to get more involved and discussed this with Alan. He suggested I might explore becoming a prison visitor, meeting up once a week or fortnight with a prisoner in the visits room at the prison. Although I welcomed this encouragement from Alan, I really wanted to use the long distance of travelling from home to the prison for more specific pastoral ministry within the jail itself.

Then things took a surprising turn. The assistant chaplain left to take up another post in the prison service. I felt that God was saying to me: "Seize this opportunity, don't let it pass."

I turned to Alan and asked: "Do you think I would ever be able to have a post as prison chaplain?" Alan had a great gift of encouragement. If he saw someone of value to the chaplaincy, he was quick of the mark to speak to them about it. Having been a full-time Church of England chaplain for twenty-eight years, he was adept at spotting someone's gift of ministry and explained why we had such a huge amount of chaplaincy volunteers and prison visitors all engaged in a variety of ministries. At this time, the senior chaplain was usually Church of England with support from Roman Catholic, Free Church and visiting ministers from other faiths.

Alan invited me into the prison to meet the rest of the chaplaincy team. I wondered how I would ever find my way around this rambling prison! After carefully unlocking and locking two gates, team member Stephen L. took me on a tour of 'A' wing, which was adjacent to the centre of the prison. As I looked around from my vantage point on landing three and surveyed the inmates, officers and general life on the wing, I imagined myself part of this community. Just what I would be doing, God had yet to reveal!

How many prisoners and who I would meet during the next years spent as a prison chaplain would indeed be a revelation. These were exciting prospects, launching into a delicate, sensitive, fast moving, expectant, sad, and hopeful ministry.

And so this was a tremendous opportunity not only for me but also for The Church of the Nazarene in the British Isles. After working as a sessional chaplain for months, the post was eventually advertised for an assistant chaplain and made into two posts. My colleague Lorna and I worked three days a week. I became the first Nazarene prison chaplain in the UK employed by the Home Office. This was new territory and a steep learning curve!

My induction service in the prison chapel was attended by The Church of the Nazarene's district superintendent, Reverend Clive Burrows, chaplain colleagues, prisoners and members of my church congregation.

God is amazing. He knew this was going to be my place of ministry for many years to come.

The prison doors had finally opened!

Chapter Three
Life in the Fast Lane

It was John Wesley, the great 18th century evangelist, who said: "I look on the entire world as my parish". At the time of writing, Lincoln prison held about seven hundred and fifty men. Being a local remand jail, there were plenty of comings and goings. I identified with the words of Wesley as I looked and saw a world of opportunity before me.

My church background was Wesleyan/Evangelical, so it was only natural to think of John Wesley and his ministry into the prisons of his day. The penal system at that time was in dire need of reform. Prisons were often inadequate to keep inmates captive so they had to be kept in irons to prevent escape. The prisons were, as a rule, damp and unsanitary. Food and water was in short supply, and the sick were not cared for or were simply left unattended. The unsanitary conditions and treatment of the sick resulted in the spread of disease to other inmates. Large numbers of people were being condemned to death for various crimes. It was a dangerous place to minister.

In fact, Wesley said, upon entering Newgate prison, "What a scene appears as soon as you enter! The very place strikes horror in your soul! How dark and dreary! How unhealthy and unclean!"

Things have moved on, thanks to the prison reformer John Howard. He visited several hundred prisons across England, Scotland, and Wales and in Europe. Following this, he published his book The State of the Prisons in 1777. It included detailed accounts of the prisons he visited, including plans, maps, and instructions for improvement. Four years earlier, an act of Parliament authorised Justices of the Peace to appoint and pay chaplains to their prisons, who had to preach two sermons every Sunday!

A notice outside every prison today reads: "Her Majesty's Prison Service serves the public by keeping in custody those committed by the courts. Our duty is to look after them with humanity and help them lead law-abiding and useful lives in custody and after release." The chaplain has a vital part to play in this statement. They are integral to the life of the prison and are involved in all aspects of the community.

It is important to remember that prisoners are people. Jails are not simply high walls, strong bars, metal doors and endless rows of cells. They are made up of people like you and I. Prisoners are not a special breed of humanity. It's always good to remember there are many more crimes committed than there are people found guilty of committing them. Their criminality apart, they are just like the rest of us, except that as a group, they seem to include more than their fair share of the disadvantaged members of society.

God had called me to minister into this unique environment, offering a ministry of reconciliation to the prisoner. Firstly with himself: an acceptance of self-recognition, then with others: family, friends, fellow prisoners, officers, staff and victims. Finally with God: repentance, conversion and discovery of God.

In the vastness of the prison, how was I going to go about this task and where was I going to start? One of the first duties of the day was to see every man who had come into the prison the day before. In the main, they came from magistrates or crown courts but other places too, such as from another prison on transfer or a licence recall. These were the usual categories but there were others. The numbers in the group could be anywhere from three to thirty, and the allotted induction time was the same regardless of number… This really was life in the fast lane!

The importance of this time, officially called an induction interview, was essential. It was a chance to make contact, gain information from the prisoner about his present condition and, if necessary, make arrangements to see the man later on.

The reasons for being in prison are varied and there were always those who didn't think they should be there. They would give many explanations, including "I was late for my probation appointment", "I've been stitched up" and "My solicitor said I would get off."

The chaplain wasn't there to pass judgment or to assess the reasons why, of course, but to deal with the situation as it presented itself. Very often, we would already know about the crime they had committed through the media. Whatever the reason for a jail sentence, it made no difference to the way the prisoner was treated. He may feel suicidal, desperate, lonely or confused. He may have left children, a pregnant wife, sick relatives or a partner unable to cope.

They too have to pick up the pieces of their lives without their loved one. The prisoner may ask me to phone his family to let them know he is well. Likewise, the family may have already rung the chaplain's office with their concerns. And not all relationships stand the test of separation. Many times I was called by one of the wing officers to support a prisoner after he had received a "Dear John" letter or being told on a domestic visit that his marriage or relationship was over.

There are many people who cannot understand why a chaplain would want to spend their time in ministering in prison. Once judgment has been made, the matter is closed for the general public. But for those involved, it is not the end. A sentence is passed and so it becomes a beginning. It will most certainly be a radical change for those who are convicted, and a huge change of life for their families and friends. It impinges on those charged with the custody of the prisoner. It will have an effect, sometimes dramatic, on the victims and their families.

The Christian does well to reflect on the words of the apostle Paul, who exhorts us to act in love and gentleness towards those who have been caught in some fault or misdeed, so we may help to bring about their restoration. This is perhaps an area where many of us struggle, either because we are indifferent or because we are ignorant of the needs of transgressors. Paul also warns us to look to our own selves and our behaviour so we may see our vulnerability and take steps to avoid temptation.

Another statutory duty was the healthcare wing of the prison. It could hold up to twenty prisoners. After being assessed, a prisoner may be placed here for personal care.

The length of stay is usually short and, according to how many men were on the wing at any one time, it is possible for the chaplain to spend a large part of the day supporting those living here.

Many prisoners had creative sides and they were encouraged to put pen to paper and draw, paint, write poetry or express their creativity in whatever way they pleased. They were in prison: with plenty of time on their hands, they were encouraged to use it productively. I have seen many wonderful paintings, drawings, writing and various pieces of craftsmanship.

I met Simon, probably aged in his late 60s. He had allegedly murdered his wife. I did not find conversation with him easy. This was not unusual, especially at a first meeting. After a while, things became easier but he never spoke about his offence. I didn't expect him to. That was his choice and personal to him. He never spoke about a faith in God until one day he handed me a piece of paper with the following written on it:

God is my help in every need;
God does my every hunger feed,
He walks beside me, guides my way,
Through every moment of the day,
I now am wise, I now am true
All things I am can do and be,
Through Christ the truth that is in me.
God is my health I can't be sick
God is my strength, unfailing, quick
Since God and love and truth are here
God and love and God is my all

I know no fear since truth is here
The infinite love of God ever enfolds me,
Bringing harmony, order and peace,
Into my mind, body and affairs.

As I read these lines, I wondered what the story of his life was and what led him to act in the way he did. Was it accident or provocation? If he was found guilty, he may never come out of prison alive. Simon was one of many who I met in similar positions.

The third task of the day was a visit to the segregation unit, otherwise known as "seg" or "block". To get there from the healthcare wing, one had to pass through two locked doors, on to A Wing, and proceed back to the centre of the prison. I was making this journey once when I all but bumped into the governor, who was giving a guided tour of the prison to the Mayor of Lincoln. It was an interesting liaison as I politely said "good morning" and attempted to move on. I always found the governor helpful and kind. He always welcomed me into his office if a problem arose, attempting to give advice and sort through issues. However, this was not the time for taking advantage of his generosity. He clearly had a timetable to work to, accompanying the mayor around this large Victorian prison. I am sure the mayor was aware of this too but he wasn't going to miss the opportunity of talking with a chaplain and was keen to know about myself and the work of the chaplaincy. I was delighted to be given this impromptu chance to speak of the ministry that God had called me to. I don't know if the mayor had a faith but he was interested to hear about mine and how I had come to be working in the prison. I looked for any signs that the Mayor was getting bored or that the governor wanted to call a halt but there was none. I've often looked back on this scenario and thanked God for this window of opportunity. I loved my job even though at times it was messy, hard, sad and painful. The other side of the coin was satisfaction in doing God's will, being the eyes, heart and feet of Jesus, moving around the prison with compassion and discernment. This was ministry "on the hoof".

The words of 1 Peter 3:15 come to mind: "But in your hearts set apart Christ as Lord. Always be prepared to give an answer to everyone who asks you to give the reason for the hope that you have. But do this with gentleness and respect" (NIV).

I carried on walking to the seg. This was a unit of twelve single cells reserved for men who caused trouble on the wing or who were there for their own protection. Some valued the isolation while others felt lonely and welcomed the chance to talk with the chaplain. On many occasions, I have been invited to pray with the prisoner in his cell. I always carried a copy of the Gideon's New Testament and psalms, and various booklets of Christian literature, which were given out on request. Very often I returned to the office empty-handed, so keen were the men to have them.

During my first year of service, I attended the prison service training centre at Newbold Revell, near Rugby. I was grateful for this opportunity to join other chaplains, working through the "Starting out" module. The information and advice given by the training officer was invaluable.

I never carried cell keys. The officers were always willing to open doors on request. Occasionally, this didn't happen if the prisoner was known to be violent or have other problems. In those circumstances, I spoke to him through the flap on the cell door. Always I was made aware if there were any concerns and, of course, my security training kicked in at times like this.

I was doing my rounds one day with the officers in the seg and thought I had seen everyone. "Wait a moment," said an officer. "You need to visit a prisoner in the special accommodation cell." I had never heard of this and wondered why it had not come to my attention before. We walked through a passage and approached a cell in the shape of a box room.

"You'll have to look through the small square window and communicate as best you can," the officer said.

I peered in and saw only a dim space. I felt frustrated as I recalled my chaplain's training: I must make some contact with the prisoner to satisfy myself that he was alive. How was I to do that in these conditions?

"Peter," I shouted, "are you alright? I can't see you?"

I turned to the officer. "I must make sure Peter is ok." I was determined by whatever means to communicate somehow.

"Look to the right", came the reply. "He's lying on his bed under a blanket." I craned my neck and could just make out a low bed and a jumble of bedding. I tried again.

"I can't see you, Peter, are you alright?" I didn't see him but I heard a muffled reply in the positive and saw the bedding move slightly. I was disheartened that I could not do more and wondered how Peter had come to be in this isolated place. By the time I next visited the seg, Peter had been moved.

In all my time in prison, I never visited this cell again, but I often wondered about Peter and what became of him. It wasn't until some years later that I happened to be on one of the wings when a prisoner approached me.

"You don't remember me," he said, "because you've never actually seen me. I was the prisoner you visited in the special accommodation cell in the seg. I could hear the conversation you had with the officers. You were so intent on making contact with me. It meant such a lot, that you went out of your way to speak to me. I have never forgotten it."

I looked at him as I recalled the incident and remembered the words of Jesus: "And whoever gives one of these little ones only a cup of cold water in the name of a disciple, assuredly I say to you, he shall by no means lose his reward" (Matthew 10:42) (NKJV). At the time I didn't seem to be offering anything much to Peter, but to him it was everything.

Alan was a good colleague, dedicated to his vocation and keen I should get as much experience in the service as possible. With his vast links in the community and churches, he was able to amass a long list of volunteers to help the chaplaincy in their various ministry roles. Part of my role was to support them in many ways. Occasionally, we would invite them into the chapel for refreshments to recognise and appreciate their work. We had an impressive group of prison visitors whose role was to visit inmates once a week. Theirs was important work. It might be that family and friends are unable to visit the prisoner in some cases, they may have disowned him. A friendly face and someone to listen can be a huge support to a lonely prisoner. Chaplaincy volunteers gave their time week after week to assist the team in prison. Other areas of ministry included supporting the chaplain at Sunday services, conducting bible studies and being part of the chaplaincy rota in the prison day by day.

During my time in the service, we developed a more rounded multi-faith team. I learned a lot through my engagement with colleagues from other faiths. The training I had at Newbold Revel was invaluable and helped me relate to prisoners of other faiths and assist them with particular requests. I eventually became employed as an ecumenical chaplain. Often, this meant nothing to the prisoner. They just wanted to see a chaplain unless, of course, they wished to see the Roman Catholic priest or Anglican priest.

I was often asked: "What do we call you?" Often when I was passing through the wings, a cheery "Hello Sister" would be heard. I smiled to myself. Prior to working in the prison, I had little contact with nuns. However, one of the first things Alan asked me to do was to make contact with The Mount, a convent in Lincoln. I spent a very nice time there, enjoying afternoon tea and meeting Sister Stephanie whom I later shared ministry with in the prison. We alternated weekly to take a short service with communion to vulnerable prisoners residing in the healthcare wing. These were intense but special times, bringing the grace of God to those who society sometimes shunned. As my ministry developed, there were many such times like this and other situations that I was called to. It was often learning and ministry on the hoof, always ready to offer a prayer to God for guidance and wisdom that what I said and did would be for His Glory.

Chapter Four
A Jail in Mourning

Chaplains are encouraged to keep contact with their faith group, which for me is the Church of the Nazarene. Its ministers meet at an annual conference and I welcomed this opportunity of meeting with colleagues to give an update about my work in the prison.

As I left the four-day conference, held in the peaceful and picturesque countryside of Derbyshire, I took the chance for reflection. Yes, I felt spiritually refreshed. I had told my story of life in prison and listened to others who had their own stories to tell of life in their churches and other places of ministry yet there was always an eagerness to get home once the conference had finished. After all, my husband, Eric was waiting for me!

I arrived home in Grimsby and relaxed with some food and a nice cup of tea. The motorway journey had been long and busy. I was starting to come down to earth and tiredness was creeping up on me. I unpacked my luggage and started to prepare for bed. Eric wouldn't be upstairs for some time; he always liked to catch the late-night news. I am more of a morning person, having to be up at about 5.30am to make the journey to the prison. It didn't take me long to drift off to sleep. No matter how cosy the bed had been at the conference centre, there's nothing to beat your own home comforts.

I woke with a start. What time was it? "Joy, Joy, get up, come quick." Eric's urgent voice called up the stairs. Was he ill? Had we been burgled? I got to the living room just as the local news came to an end on the television.

"What on earth is the matter?" I asked.

"You have just missed it," Eric replied. "There's a riot at Lincoln prison. Personnel are being drafted in from other prisons to help with the crisis. It looks like a serious matter."

That was the only information I had. As it was late at night, there was little I could do but wait for further news from the senior chaplain, Alan, and the Prison Service. I had a fitful night's sleep as I wondered about the TV report and the extent of the damage. It never occurred to me that something like a riot could ever take place!

The following morning, there was little news by way of the media. Eventually Alan rang.

"There has been trouble in the jail," he said. "A riot started on 'A' wing and moved to 'B' and 'E'. Come over. I will meet you at the main gate and we will assess the situation to see what we can do."

I set off from home not knowing what would lie ahead. I wasn't given any details as to the extent of the damage, or the health of the prisoners or staff.

Alan was waiting at the gate. There were several police vans, and staff coming and going, but this was like any other working day. We checked in and walked across the yard, which was strewn with more litter than normal. We entered the prison on the ground floor to access 'A' wing and the

43

chaplaincy office. I noticed more litter and clutter but most of all, I was aware of a silence and stillness that was almost unreal. Prison is usually a place of hustle and bustle. Even behind closed doors you get a sense of what's happening on the wings as men prepared for the day's activities. Not today. It was as though time stood still.

As Alan was about to put his key in the lock, the duty governor for the day appeared. "Watch where you are walking when you get on the wing," he told us. "There's lots of debris, water and mess about. I'm not sure what state the chaplaincy office is in. Mind how you go."

Off we went, I walking cautiously behind Alan. We stepped onto the wing and stopped in our tracks. The scene was one of utter devastation. What was once a place of order and discipline was now carnage and filth.

A feeling of dismay, confusion and disbelief swept over me as I surveyed the wreckage of a wing that once had been home to nearly two hundred men. No one was around now to shout out that familiar cheery greeting of "Good morning, miss, how you are?" All was quiet apart from the hushed activity of a small group of people on landing two. Did I catch sight of a police officer standing on guard outside one of the cells? I learned later the dismal truth of his presence.

For the moment, Alan and I focused on doing what we could to salvage anything out of the mess and picked our way through three more locked gates to the chaplaincy office. Miraculously, the office had not been entered and apart from having no electric light, we were able to see enough to access anything needed to enable us to carry on with our chaplaincy work. Knowing where to start was the question.

The BBC reported that the destruction at HMP Lincoln in October 2002 was the worst disturbance at a British jail for 11 years. Sometime later, when those responsible were brought before the courts, the judge sentenced 21 inmates for prison mutiny, assault, unlawful wounding and violent disorder–totalling 97 years in jail. He said: "There was anarchy and mayhem. The prison was in the hands of the prisoners for about eight hours". He added: "The mayhem was the worst in England since the riot at HM Strangeways, Manchester, in 1990."

At earlier hearings, prosecutor Gordon Aspden told how the riot was planned by a group being held on the jail's 'A' wing. They overpowered a guard and stole his cell keys. The rioters rampaged to the sex offenders' wing, where some feigned death as the rioters exploded oxygen cylinders in an attempt to blow open cell doors. Mr Aspden said: "There was discontent about changes to the prison menu and the introduction of sandwiches at lunchtime. A group of ringleaders were responsible for starting the trouble but once the mutiny was in progress, other inmates took the opportunity to join in. It was sheer lawlessness. There were numerous assaults on other prisoners and everything that came to hand was damaged or destroyed. Absolutely no mercy was shown. For over eight hours, the prison was in the hands of the inmates. It was anarchy." Some 168 prison riot officers, brought in from jails up to 150 miles away, regained control at 4am.

The daily life and regime of the prison was clearly inoperable. With this in mind, Alan and I stepped back on to what remained of 'A' wing. As we looked again at the carnage, many thoughts and emotions ran through my mind and despair shivered down my spine. There were many questions as yet unanswered. Perhaps they never would be.

But I remembered the promise of God in Deuteronomy 31:8: "The Lord Himself goes before you and will be with you and will never leave you nor forsake you. Do not be afraid, and do not be discouraged" (NIV). With those words to sustain me, I bravely went forward to face life in the aftermath.

The only way we could carry out our work was to face what lay before our eyes. The little bit of information we picked up suggested that although most of the men on the wing had been shipped out to other prisons during the night, a few remained in cells that still had a door attached. The remaining men were in cells that had no name and number card on the outside, or the name card had been switched during the riots and the details did not match. We surveyed the task before us and painstakingly picked our way through debris to access the cells. Other chaplains had been contacted so extra help was on the way. The immediate task was to reassure those left that help and assistance was coming. None were allowed out of their cells and the doors were unlocked only under extreme circumstances. Instead of going to the servery area for meals, sandwiches were brought to them, and officers opened up with caution.

After all cells on the ground floor were visited and checked for anyone present, I looked up to what lay on landings two, three and four. Two stairways led to landing two. One was completely destroyed and lay on a heap, demolished. The second looked reasonably intact. I arrived at the top of the stairway. To my right was the group of people I observed earlier and I now was able to see more.

The police were there and a cell was cordoned off. Clearly a death had occurred. Sometime later, at a four-day inquest, I learned that 37-year-old Lee Blake, from Scunthorpe, had died from a drugs overdose. A jury returned a verdict of death by misadventure. The BBC reported that "Lee had locked himself in his cell to take refuge from the trouble". The inquest also heard that comatose prisoners were "scattered everywhere" after either taking drugs or being attacked. The drugs had been looted from the pharmacy. In addition to Lee's death, 35 prisoners needed hospital treatment and so did some officers.

Prison officer Nick Scott, who rescued a colleague from being attacked by rioting inmates, won a Queen's Commendation for Bravery. Nick managed to haul his seriously injured colleague from a cell full of masked prisoners. He recalled: "I heard a noise but didn't really know whether it was him or a prisoner. I saw he had blood pouring from his head, lying on the floor with a number of masked inmates around him, all wearing balaclavas and carrying some sort of weaponry, such as a bed leg or a table leg. I shouted to another officer to hit the general alarm bell. When I entered the cell to try to get to Dave [the injured officer] I was forced back and a fight ensured. A lot of people went through a horrific time that night, officers and inmates. I was doing my job and I would do it again tomorrow and I would expect anyone else to do the same."

The Guardian newspaper reported that "police from five counties surrounded the prison to prevent a break-out and a no-fly zone above the prison was declared. It is expected to be weeks before the 200 places that have been lost can be brought back into use, putting increased pressure on a prison system already considered close to breaking point."

Despite the riot and its devastating effect, work had to go on as best it could. With a limited regime and heightened security, combined with supporting staff and covering some away on sick leave, the chaplaincy team had more than enough to do. This was the nature of our role: to offer support, a friendly face, a listening ear, and prayers to be a quiet presence in time of need can speak volumes.

I thought about Jesus in His day and how He looked out on the crowds and had compassion for them. I felt that same compassion as I surveyed the state of the jail and all who worked there. But this had to be mixed with a strong determination and faith in the God that I knew was more than able to help in time of need. There would be numerous occasions over the next weeks—and indeed for the eleven years that I worked as a chaplain—that I would be calling on Him and inviting others to do so also.

Chapter Five
Picking up the Pieces

Finding a place of quiet in the prison was not always easy but the chapel offered respite and calm. It was used for services and various groups throughout the week. Prisoners would often request to go to the chapel to light a candle on hearing news of the death of a loved one. And because it was such a large area, the prison governor would occasionally hold staff meetings there.

On entering the chapel, I quickly realised the riot had affected the whole prison in one way or another. Routine, as we knew it, had been severely impacted and allowances had to be made for disruption in every department... including the chapel.

As I turned the key to enter, I looked over the vast expanse in amazement. What had been going on in here? The chapel had clearly been used as a base for prison officers and staff to conduct their meetings, and as a place to rest and eat during and after the disturbances. I guess they had more pressing things to do than keep the chapel tidy. Normally a chapel orderly would clean the space, but not at the moment! Ah well, I could pray as I went around picking up empty food containers, drink cartons, jackets and coats.

And what was that? One shoe. Where was the other? I never did find it!

I couldn't imagine how officers and staff at the forefront of the disturbances felt. Many of them came from military backgrounds and this, together with Prison Service training, would leave them well equipped to handle trouble. Nevertheless, as in any conflict, there is always the unknown and unexpected waiting to happen. Understandably, many staff were traumatised, but specialised help and counselling was at hand, including support from the chaplaincy team. We were kept very busy, not only with staff at work but also home visits for those on sick leave.

And then there were the 32 prisoners at Lincoln County Hospital, across the road from the prison. They were too sick to be moved to other jails at this time. They may have been injured during the riot or taken substances to make themselves unwell.

I accompanied the duty governor one day to visit these men, who were contained with officers on one long ward. As a group, they looked a sorry sight! We sought to establish the condition of their health and whether they had any other immediate concerns that the governor or I could deal with. It was highly sensitive stuff, as some of them may have been instigators of the riot. That aside, they were human beings with needs and feelings, just like the rest of us.

And what about me? How did I feel? The few remaining prisoners on 'A' wing were eventually moved and the wing was shut down prior to its eventual refurbishment. It was as I looked over the empty wing that I felt an immense sense of grief and sadness. The sudden departure of men on a wing that had recently been full to capacity, some of whom I had been supporting and counselling in various situations, was overwhelming. There was Tony on landing four and all those prayers we shared together, the bible passages we read, intense conversations we had. Where had he gone? He was in such a vulnerable condition. I hated to think of his state now.

Mick on the threes; I'd miss his cheery greeting. Dave on the ones; he'd only just arrived. What about the families? How were they coping, not knowing the full extent of what had taken place? So many questions that may never have an answer!

The days working in the prison and paying home visits filled much of the week. As chaplains, we were encouraged to look after ourselves and have our own support systems. In essence, this was good sound advice. Practically, it didn't always work efficiently. Of course people meant well, but unless one has worked in a prison, it's hard to relate to life on the inside. But folk prayed for me and that meant everything. Days off were spent catching up with jobs at home or spending relaxing time with Eric. That was easier said than done, as thoughts of the prison crowded my mind.

One day the phone rang. "Hello Joy, how are you? I've been thinking about you working in the prison, especially with the recent riot that has taken place."

I recognised the voice straight away. It was an elderly retired church minister who lived in Yorkshire. From previous conversations, I knew that his many years of experience in ministry had at times been with ex-offenders or visiting in prison. Immediately, he had a handle on my situation. As our conversation flowed, he knew exactly what I and others had gone through. It was good to have a listening ear from someone who understood the complexities of what had taken place. As we chatted away, he suddenly said:

"Joy, you need to talk to someone. I can tell by the tone of your voice and the quickness of your speech that perhaps you are feeling the strain."

For a moment, I was taken aback but I couldn't deny that he was right. I took him at his word and found people I knew would have empathy and give me support. And there is someone who understands us all, no matter who we are, whatever we have done or what situation we are in.

Jesus said: "Come to Me, all you who labour and are heavy laden, and I will give you rest. Take my yoke upon you and learn from me, for I am lowly in heart and you will find rest for your souls" (Matt. 11:28-29) (NJKV).

I knew all along that Jesus was with me but nevertheless, we are all human and need the support of others from time to time.

As 'A' wing was fairly near the chaplaincy office, it was difficult not to be reminded of the riot until eventually, the wing was sealed off and refurbishment work began. Day by day, we could hear and see progress being made, until finally, all was quiet. The work was complete and 'A' wing was restored. It was unveiled to reveal four landings of new bright, clean, gleaming renewed cells. It was quite some time before the wing opened and once again, prisoners called for the chaplain. In the meantime, the wing stood empty: a stark reminder of what had taken place. It was a hopeful time but I couldn't help wondering what I would feel like when I once again stepped onto the wing. Would my heart be filled with grief and sadness? Would there be a sense of unfinished business? I decided to take action. Choosing a time when it was relatively quiet, I took the stairs to the top floor, unlocked the gate and stepped onto landing four of 'A' wing. Once a hive of activity, the wing stood motionless; sunshine beamed through the windows as though a light had been switched on and for a moment, I almost forgot that the riot had started here. Those responsible had put their own lives at risk and those of many others. One person died and many were injured, physically and emotionally.

I walked along the landing, observing every space was on view. Paintwork shone and fitments gleamed. I intentionally took my time, praying as I went, that peace would be bestowed on the prison and particularly this wing when it reopened. I was undisturbed so I continued to landings three, two and one, praying as I went. I had faith to believe that God had heard my prayers and that He would bring healing and wholeness to my soul and all who had been affected. I went on my way with a renewed hope for the future.

The whole prison had been affected by the riot and although other wings were not damaged in the same way as 'A' wing, incidents had taken place and tensions were high. A lot of men were traumatised, living in a state of agitation. This was felt keenly on 'E' wing, which was classed for vulnerable prisoners. Some of the men here had committed sex offences. Rioters tried to gain access to these men in their cells, causing them to fear for their lives. There was slight damage to the wing but no one was hurt. 'B' and 'C' wings were relatively unscathed. But this reduced regime for many months and little activity.

During this time, a request came from a prisoner on 'C' wing. Dave was a likeable man whom I had spoken to several times. As always, I carried with me Gideon's New Testament and Psalms bible and a few diaries to hand out if needed. This was probably what he wanted. The entire wing was locked down and it would be unlikely I'd be able to speak in private with Dave.

I enlisted the help of an officer patrolling the landings. To my surprise, he looked through Dave's cell door flap and turned the key. He asked Dave to step outside and then stood a suitable distance away from us.

"What can I help you with, Dave?" I asked. Without further ado, he said: "I am being released tomorrow and really want things to work out with my wife in our marriage. Can you give me a blessing?"

He dropped onto his knees. It was a profound and spiritual moment, on a landing full of prisoners behind closed doors and not another soul about; just the three of us. I put my hands on Dave's head and prayed over him while also thanking God for this moment of opportunity. Dave got up, shook my hand and went back in his cell. In the silence of these moments, God's presence is felt. It was a Holy encounter, a divine meeting.

The future included a new managing Anglican chaplain, Reverend Jeff Bird. I was sorry to see Alan leave the Prison Service, but retirement came. I will always be immensely grateful that he helped, encouraged and trained me in prison chaplaincy. In what could sometimes be a difficult and hostile environment, he pushed to make things happen. His life's work was in the service and this was reflected in the way he handled situations.

With a new chaplain came a new chaplaincy office, as the old one had been temporary due to refurbishments, and we all had to have computer training. Our team also expanded to include an Imam and other faith chaplains. This was now a multi-faith team. We were a good one and worked well together, and there was much to learn of other faiths. Training was done in-house and at the Prison Service's college. It was essential and reminded me that understanding someone's culture and faith leads to a greater tolerance, not only in prison but also in our communities.

Jeff, like Alan, had extensive experience and had worked in several prisons around the country. He was a very kind man with an eye for detail, always affirming the chaplains in his team. He soon established a routine for the chaplains according to each one's ministry strengths.

Working in a prison chaplaincy demands you are conversant with and have a working understanding of all the major faiths. The starting point is the definition of faith and faiths. What do they mean? How is faith different from religion and culture? As part of our training, we visited The Forest Hermitage in Warwickshire. We were given a tour and a talk on the Buddhist faith, followed by a question-and-answer session. It was most informative and a starting place to continue learning. We also visited a Sikh Gurdwara. The temple was impressive and contained a Langer Hall for free vegetarian food for all, to demonstrate hospitality. It also had a library, nursery and classroom. Ladies wore head scarves as we toured the temple and sat in its exquisite surroundings. The Hindu chaplain also gave us an informative talk about Hinduism.

Back in the prison, I completed training in Islam with the Imam Chaplain, who invited me to Lincoln's mosque. Before entering I took off my shoes and covered my head. I observed, while those present said their prayers and the Imam then gave me a tour, explaining the meaning of various worship aids and artefacts.

I came to realise how important it was to learn about other faiths, especially working in a multi-faith chaplaincy. It also meant that more chaplains were available to meet the needs of the prisoners. All chaplains were expected to carry out generic duties as well as faith-specific requests. Our Imam worked full-time and gave a lot of time and care to prisoners who were of other faiths or none. I also took the opportunity to continue training by engaging with prisoners of faith to determine what they considered was faith and what was culture. I learned so much in this way that I can truly say my life and faith was enriched in the process.

Respect for another person, regardless of faith, is of intricate worth. While many despise the prisoner, we might reflect on the following prayer:

Almighty and everlasting God,

You hate nothing that you have made and forgive the sins of all who are penitent. Create and make in us new and contrite hearts, that, lamenting our sins and acknowledging our wretchedness, we may receive from you, the God of all mercy, perfect forgiveness and peace; through Jesus Christ our Lord.

(The Alternative Service Book, 1990)

Chapter Six
'What a Difference a Day Makes'

"What a difference a day makes," to quote the words of a popular song.

Although prison is structured with various timetables and regimes, it often seems as though every day is pretty much the same. The reality is that things can change in a moment.

To some prisoners, the appearance of a chaplain seeking them out can spell doom and gloom. Is it bad news? Has some one died? Sadly in many cases, this is so. Serving a prison sentence, separated from family; especially long sentences, will mean just that. Supporting someone through bereavement can be a long and difficult process. Doing the best we can for the prisoner and his family is a sensitive and important ministry.

News came to the chaplaincy office of the death of a prisoner's mother. After verifying that the details were correct, I found Trevor at work in one of the prison's workshops. I'd never met him before but showed his religion was registered as Church of England. Often this information was given when the inmate first arrived, and could be true or false. In Trevor's case, I had yet to find out.

In the workshop, about 40 men were busily engaged in their tasks. For many it was painting and I was impressed with the quality of work produced here. Many men where gifted in this craft and paintings were displayed on the walls. Some were available to buy and on occasion displayed in exhibitions in the community. Trevor was brought to meet me in a quiet room.

It is never easy imparting bad news and one has to be prepared for changing reactions and emotions. What would this meeting bring? I invited Trevor to sit down and I broke the news to him. I gave all the details I had. There was silence for a considerable length of time. Eventually, I asked if he or his family had any religious faith. He spoke fondly of going to the Salvation Army Sunday School as a child. All was quiet again until eventually, Trevor said: "Would you like to see my paintings?" It seemed as though Trevor didn't want or need to talk any more about his mother's death. I said yes and he produced his portfolio of some of the most beautiful paintings I had ever seen. My eyes came to rest upon the scene of a thatched cottage surrounded by trailing roses on a trellis with plants and flowers in abundance. The garden gate opened onto a lane leading down to a church in the background. The pastel colours were delicate and easy on the eye. Trevor had captured the scene beautifully and was not slow to notice how this picture had caught my attention. "Would you like to have it?" he asked.

I was taken aback, but couldn't deny it would look very nice on my lounge wall at home. I was mindful that receiving anything from a prisoner was not an accepted practice, let alone taking something out of the prison. However, when I made the request, the prison agreed to the gift. The picture hangs in my home today, a reminder of Trevor and the many men I had the privilege of ministering to in prison.

After risk assessments, Trevor was not allowed to attend his mother's funeral. This sometimes happens with prisoners of a certain category. Trevor accepted this and I made sure he got extra support during this time. He didn't want to go to the chapel or have prayers, so I handed him bereavement leaflets in the hope he would gain some comfort.

It was a very different story a year later. News came that Trevor's wife, aged in her late 30s, had died suddenly. When he was told he would be unable to attend the funeral service, he was distraught. Although I understood his anguish, it was no use speaking up on his behalf as the nature of his offence would have had some bearing on the decision.

We did the best we could for him in his sorrow. The men on the wing raised almost £100 to have a wreath sent on their behalf, which I ordered for them through a local florist. It was an extremely sad occasion. The prison authorities said Trevor could visit his wife's grave some weeks after, and he requested that I help him choose a suitable poem to read at the graveside. He returned sad, but in a much calmer frame of mind, knowing that at least he had been able to do something. The officers who escorted Trevor to the grave were very sensitive, kind and caring.

We all like to feel we are in control of our lives and make our own decisions. For the prisoner, this is very restricted, but the chaplain can sometimes make a difference by speaking on the prisoner's behalf and finding ways round and through situations that previously appeared insurmountable.

"My brother is in the prison and his mother is very ill with cancer and not expected to live much longer. Could you assist in helping him to put in a request to the governor to visit her?" I noted the details from Keith's sister and assured her I would do all I could to help, but that it would be the governor's decision.

In cases of serious illness or death, verifying the facts with the appropriate authority is not always easy. If the death is already in the hands of a funeral director, then a telephone call will usually confirm this. Because of the data protection act, in other cases obtaining the facts are more difficult. It can be frustrating in attempting to clarify the details. Staff at hospitals and GPs' surgeries are hesitant in giving out information. Of course, it works both ways: prison staff should not give out confidential information relating to the prison and prisoners, either.

In the case of Keith's mother, we gained information from her GP and district nurses. Time was running out. I helped Keith fill out the application to visit his mother. How would his security check be? Would the governor sanction it? Would there be prison officers available to escort Keith? After all, Manchester was quite a distance from Lincoln.

But yes, it was all systems go and the visit went ahead. I made a point of seeing Keith when he returned. He was very emotional; after all, he would not see his mother alive again. He had nothing but praise for the officers who escorted him. He told me how kind and considerate they were. They, with the family, sent out for fish and chips and enjoyed a meal before the return journey. It wasn't an easy day for Keith or his family but all in a day's work for me. I was touched to receive a thank-you card from Keith's family, part of which reads: "Thank you very much for helping to arrange my brother's (Keith's) home visit. It helped him a great deal."

We are all on a journey through life. Within reason, for many of us we are in a position to control where and how we live. Not so for the prisoner. His choices are limited and decisions are often made for him. However, life can take on meaning—even in prison. As a Christian minister, I was privileged to help men who expressed an interest in the Christian faith to explore Christianity and either rekindles a lapsed faith or to find for the first time that it had meaning. As a chaplaincy, we were able to offer bible study groups, Alpha courses exploring Christianity, and worship services that often included church groups from the community. These groups faithfully and regularly came into the prison. The men appreciated seeing new faces and people who took an interest in them and their welfare. There was an abundance of Christian literature to be had too—all for free!

Gerry arrived from a local court. It was his first time inside. As always, we took extra care with those men who had not been in prison before. Gerry was a likeable and pleasant man in his mid-30s. At first glance, it was hard to see why he had ended up here. However, here he was, and like all other men, he had our support.

At the initial introduction to chaplaincy services, Gerry said he had no particular faith but that his late parents were Salvationists and possibly some of their faith had rubbed off on him. He had never owned a bible or seen the Gideon's New Testament and Psalms, and was pleased to accept it.

A few days passed before I saw Gerry again. How talkative he was. He appeared to be adapting to life in prison and was being relocated to another wing. "Is there a chapel service I can go to?" he asked. "I have been reading my New Testament and Psalms and would like to go." "Certainly," I replied, and added his name to the list. From then on, he attended regularly and also went to education classes in the week to improve his reading and writing. Apart from a few health problems troubling him from time to time, Gerry settled well and his new-found Christian faith meant a lot to him.

We were well into December and life was extra busy, preparing for Christmas carol services and special events. The highlight of the season was always the Christmas carol concert. This was attended by the governor, the High Sherriff of Lincolnshire and invited guests such as the community groups who supported Sunday services and bible studies. Everyone participating in the concert busied themselves learning and practising songs or readings. This included Gerry who, by now, was a faithful attendee of services. His eagerness to take part in the concert was rewarded with a piece of scripture to read. His enthusiasm was infectious and everyone was amazed at how well he was doing. His determination was helped by God, whom he had come to rely on over the weeks and months.

One day, news came that Gerry had been admitted to Lincoln County Hospital. Despite his health issues, I found him in good spirits. His main concern was to recover sufficiently enough to be discharged in time for the carol concert. He requested a bible to carry on practising the reading. I ensured this, and prayed that his recovery would be swift. He was in hospital a while longer and on each visit, I was amazed to see his radiant face, and how he would read his bible with relish.

He then said: "I'm not ashamed for anyone to know I am a Christian." I thought back to his first day in prison and looked at him now. The words of the apostle Paul came to mind:

"Therefore, if anyone is in Christ, he is a new creation: old things have passed away; behold all things have become new" (2 Corinthians 5:17) (NKJV).

The carol concert arrived and sure enough, Gerry was there, complete with bible, and stood proudly reading his appointed scripture. What an amazing transformation and testimony of what God can do in someone's life—even a prisoner!

1. What a difference a day makes by Dinah Washington. Produced by Clyde Otis 1959

Chapter Seven
Amazing Grace

The hymn 'Amazing Grace' was written by John Newton. He was involved in the slave trade and during a severe storm at sea, he had a revelation experience of God, turned to Him in repentance and wrote this hymn. It is still popular today, sung at church services, funerals, football matches and many other places. This well-known hymn has brought many people to faith in God.

Richard Foster quotes: "Grace saves us from life without God... even more it empowers us for life with God."[1]

In prison, many men come to faith in God. In fact I've often heard these words said: "Perhaps I had to come into prison to find God." It's true in society also. Perhaps a tragedy happens and we turn to God in our despair, or in some cases we may reject Him totally as the One who has not helped us when we needed it most. Or at least that's how we interpret it! Whichever way we look at it, adversity can be a stepping stone to finding God.

Of course, there are those people who will say: "It's alright turning to God in prison but on release many will return to their old lifestyles."

We can't deny that this is true in some cases. The first 24 hours after release can literally mean make or break for some prisoners. The work of community chaplaincies, prison fellowships and other groups who can meet the newly-released prisoner as soon as he steps outside the gate is invaluable. After serving a sentence, however long or short, the world can seem a strange and unwelcome place. Old associates may be waiting to lure them back to old lifestyles. It's easy to condemn those who return to prison time and time again, but how do we know what sort of life awaits them on the outside? Until we have walked a mile in someone else's shoes, we can't possibly know what fears, temptations, heartaches, anxieties or apprehensions they grapple with.

The court has judged someone guilty; sentence has been passed and time served. But that's not the end of the matter. Often society doesn't want to accept an ex-offender. Integration back into community is hard without support. For those who have become Christians and expressed a desire to attend church on release, contact with a vicar or church fellowship prior to release is essential and can lead to a good future and informed lifestyle choices. I've known many hardened criminals find God in prison and go on to be evangelists, ministers and authors, leading many others to accept Jesus as Saviour.

Author Philip Yancey said: "I rejected the church for a time because I found so little grace there. I returned because I found grace nowhere else." [2]

Part of the role of a chaplain is walking alongside those who the courts have committed to prison. What a mixed bunch! There are familiar faces who return time after time, as I discovered one winter's morning. I had a long drive from home to the prison. In good weather it was a pleasant journey and relatively easy, with places of interest along the way. Farmhouses and small holdings signs outside offering their goods for sale. Fresh vegetables and fruit could be brought cheaply, payment being left in an honesty box by the roadside. Bedding out plants, broad beans, beetroot, flowers, strawberries in the summer… it was a real treat.

It was nearing Christmas when I noticed the sign: "Order your free-range Christmas turkey now." I had passed this smallholding many times and seen the chickens and turkeys running about. This is too good to miss, I thought. The next time I passed, I pulled in and ordered a suitably sized turkey in readiness for Christmas dinner. "It should be ready two days before Christmas," they said. "That's all right," I replied, "I will pick it up on my way home from the prison on my last working day before Christmas." But when I stopped again, it wasn't ready. Oh dear, I thought, it's going to be a Christmas Eve journey to fetch it. My accommodating husband, Eric, drove over to collect it. As we tucked in on Christmas Day, we agreed it was the best turkey we had ever tasted.

The winter weather turned bad over Christmas, giving way to heavy snow in some parts with ice and very cold winds. It was not pleasant driving back to work after the break. I managed to keep going without any major mishaps and arrived at the prison one morning, cold and wet with the wintry snow. I saw a familiar face: Ronnie was back in prison. We met as the snow swirled around the already covered yard. "Hello Miss," he said, holding out his hand

and shaking mine enthusiastically. He then leaned forward and kissed me softly on the cheek.

It wasn't the first time I'd had a close encounter with a prisoner. Of course, there has to be an awareness and integrity with any physical contact, but I looked on this as a divine moment of God's presence on a bleak morning that warmed both of our hearts.

Christmas in jail can be hard when inmates are separated from their loved ones. The Prison Service tries to make it as festive and pleasant as possible. There are activities on the wings and a traditional Christmas lunch and tea for those who want it. The annual carol concert in the chapel is well attended by prisoners and volunteers. The promise of mince pies afterwards is always a reason to attend!

It was not long into the New Year when I entered the chaplaincy office just as the phone started ringing. A softly spoken female voice was on the line. Mary was the mother of one of the prisoners, Paul. Her voice faltered as she told how her estranged husband had died in tragic circumstances.

Although she lived in Merseyside, she wanted to break the news to Paul in person and asked if I could be present. On the day of her visit, we were allocated a side room. It is usual for staff to be extra vigilant in cases of bereavement or news of anything serious as it can make the prisoner feel vulnerable, even suicidal. I noted Mary's sleight frame and fragile state, and greeted her warmly. Soon after, Paul entered the room and hugged his mother. After Mary delivered her devastating news, it was hard to tell how Paul took it. It had been some considerable time since he'd had contact with his father. They chatted over family business and Mary asked if Paul would be allowed to attend the funeral. Time went on and the visit drew to a close. Thinking that mother and son would like some time alone, I asked, "Shall I wait outside the room?" "Oh no," Mary said, "Please stay, I want to ask you something." I was curious "Would you conduct the funeral service please?" Experience had taught me to choose my words carefully, while answering quickly and honestly. This was the first time I had been asked to conduct a funeral service for a prisoner's relative but as with any funeral I had always accepted, I believe it is a privilege to be entrusted with it. No matter what the situation was now, I was pretty sure that love would have been shared in that family at one time. I didn't hesitate in accepting. We said our goodbyes and I got down to the business of checking funeral details, filling out forms, taking it to the security department for their checks and then on to the governor for his approval.

Prior to the funeral, I paid a pastoral visit to Paul's sister and her family. They lived in Boston where the funeral was being held. They were a pleasant family and Paul's sister recalled the good upbringing they had. Holidays were remembered with fondness and I built up a picture of life with their dad and one of him as a person. Ties in recent years had become fragmented but there is always a positive side to every story. I asked if there were any particular hymns they would like. She said her father had not been particularly religious but said he liked Amazing Grace. I smiled to myself but didn`t say a word!

The day of the funeral arrived. The service was at 9.30am and Eric accompanied me. Although Eric had never been into the prison or had contact with inmates, he was very supportive, reminding me of important meetings, phone calls to return and places to go.

We arrived at the crematorium car park. It was empty apart from two cars, one with a male inside. I started to think about the situation we were in. Some may say my brain was overreacting but we were expecting a prisoner. He would be handcuffed to two officers, together with any other security measures deemed necessary. I believed Paul was a low-risk prisoner but how could we account for who would be attending the funeral? Who was that lone man in the car park? Security, surveillance, funeral attender, council worker, or none of these? "Hang on," I told myself, "get a grip, you will be a nervous wreck and won't be able to conduct the service if you don't get things in perspective."

To be on the safe side, I took Eric with me into the crematorium and suggested he wait in the vestry. But where was the vestry? There didn't appear to be any crematorium staff about. I walked down a long corridor to find a clerk at her desk. As if by magic, an attendant appeared and showed me into the vestry, which was nicely equipped with everything I might need. I left Eric reading the morning paper and went into the chapel, spoke with the person in charge of music and got my books and papers in order on the lectern. All systems go.

I waited at the door for the funeral party to arrive. I didn't expect a large gathering, just close family and friends. I greeted them warmly. This wasn't an easy time, dealing with their own grief and seeing Paul in handcuffs. But, on the positive side, he had been given permission to attend. It was a long drive from Lincoln to Boston and I hoped he and the officers accompanying him would be on time. They were.

The service began. Rather than singing Amazing Grace, we walked into the chapel to hear it being played. It was a good way to start and reminded us that God was with us, and His presence filled the room with His grace and mercy. I looked out on the family and thought: "Why does life get so complicated and fragmented?" People die alone; end up in prison and families break up. However we look at it, at least this family came together irrespective of their current situation. They were united in grief. Perhaps the events of this day might lead them to a better future.

Once the service finished, the party made their way out. I shook their hands and hovered in the background until they eventually went on their way. Only then could I breathe a sigh of relief that it had gone according to plan. However, the mourners were hesitant in moving off.

One of the prison officers approached me and asked if there was a private room where Paul and his mother could spend a few minutes together. I was unfamiliar with the building and wasn't sure how the staff would react. I didn't feel inclined to ask them. However, there was a way round this as long as Paul, the officers and his mother didn't come into contact with staff or members of the public. All seemed to be quiet. "Follow me," I said, walking quickly back to the vestry. This would be the perfect room as long as I could get Eric out. They followed and I flung the vestry door open. The look on Eric's face was a picture as he jumped at my sudden entrance.

"Quick, the prisoner and his mother want to use this room for a few minutes." He looked astonished as I disrobed, gathered my bag and books in double-quick time and led him out. "All yours," I said. I didn't want Eric to be put in a compromising position so he returned to the car and I waited until everyone had left the building. As it happened, it remained as quiet as when I had first arrived.

It was a sensitive touch to conclude the proceedings of the morning. I came away knowing how kind the officers had been and realised how precious our time on this earth is, how important it is to maintain relationships and try to achieve reconciliation whenever possible, keeping lines of communication open. Eric and I took the opportunity to shop in Boston. As we mingled with other shoppers, I doubted whether any of them had experienced such an interesting morning.

"Give us the Grace to accept with serenity the things that cannot be changed, courage to change the things that should be changed and the wisdom to know the one from the other." (Richard Niebuhr).

1. Celebration of Discipline by Richard J. Foster. Published by Hodder and Stoughton 2008.
2. What's so amazing about Grace by Philip Yancey. Published by Harper Collins 1997.

Chapter Eight
Everything Has Its Time

Everything has its time," says the Portuguese proverb.

This saying takes me back to the swinging Sixties and the song by The Byrd's called 'Turn, Turn, Turn', which is based on chapter three of the Old Testament book of Ecclesiastes: "To everything there is a season, a time for ever purpose under heaven" (NJKV).

Whatever a day holds for us, we can be sure that time will keep rolling wherever we are. The prisoner may be marking days off on his calendar, keeping his release date firmly in mind. In the case of a long sentence, time may be hanging heavy in his hands.

When I started work as a prison chaplain in 2001, I read the words of St. Paul in his letter to the Ephesians, in which he says, "We are to be Imitators of God, Children of light, being careful how we live and to make the most of the time."

Throughout my prison ministry, I endeavoured to heed these words. There is a saying that inmates are "doing time". The aim of the Prison Service is to ensure that offenders are spending time in purposeful activity and pursuing resources that will help them not re-offend, aiding their resettlement back into society.

There's one thing for sure: in the prison, I never had time on my hands; it might have looked that way sometimes as I was standing by the meal queue at lunch or teatime. This was an opportunity to be seen and available for anyone who wanted a brief chat or to catch up with someone whom I had intended to speak with during the day but had not managed it. There could have been numerous reasons why that had not happened. The prisoner may have been on domestic or legal visits, been out to court or at an outside hospital appointment. He could have just returned from a funeral of a close relative. The reasons were many. Keeping as updated as possible with the life of the prison is important. The confidential role of a chaplain is much valued. However, there are occasions when it is necessary to record or share information if the prisoner is thought to be at risk of self-harm or a security threat.

Chaplains, along with all prison staff, are expected to keep a record of their working day. There are occasions when it is difficult to quantify the role of a chaplain. Being available and accessible to all is vital but how this is worked out is varied and complex. There are occasions when, despite the best efforts of staff, someone takes their own life. At times like this, it's hard to reconcile "A time for every purpose under heaven." Was this intentional or an accident? There is always an inquiry, inquest and support for the deceased's family and the staff.

A call came through on the radio that an incident had taken place on 'E' wing. There was a flurry of activity, so I kept a discreet distance from the cell in question but got the feeling that things were not looking good. In practical terms, there was nothing I could do. The rest of the wing was still, apart from this cell where a cordon was erected for security and privacy. This was a very sad day. I did not know the prisoner nor had any contact with him. I could have left the scene but no—my place was here.

An incident of this nature affects the whole prison and I might be called on at any time to offer support. As it happened, I wasn't, but nevertheless there I remained until I felt the time was right to leave.

I returned to the chaplaincy and reflected on the morning's events, making a note in the daily journal. What had I done with the time spent on the wing? Only God knew the answer to that. "To everything there is a season, a time for every purpose under heaven."

It was some weeks later that an internal confidential letter arrived for me "What could this mean?" I thought anxiously. I scanned the contents and noted the signature at the bottom was of a senior member of staff. It was a letter of thanks about the suicide on 'E' wing and noted that staff had appreciated me being present by the cell of the deceased. I was moved; after all, I was only doing my job. It reminded me how delicate the chaplain's role is. Having the wisdom to discern the mood of the moment and if any action should be taken is crucial, whether this involves prisoners or not. If I hadn't known before, I learned again that the value of a chaplain's presence has far-reaching effects. Time had moved on, but someone that day may have realised God does care, even in the midst of our tragedies.

It was 4.30pm, so time for reviewing the day's work, making sure everything had been recorded, emails sent, messages left, phone calls made; all in order for another day. I tidied up and prepared to put my coat on. By the time I was ready to leave, it would be 5pm…if things went smoothly. Although the prison is spread over a large estate, every part must function efficiently. An incident in the prison possibly results in a lockdown or, at least, measures taken to ensure everything and everybody is safe before normal service resumes. If you happen to be at the gate when this happens, there is nothing you can do but wait for the all-clear before being allowed to leave the prison.

On this particular evening, I had just put one arm in my coat sleeve when the phone rang. The voice on the other end sounded familiar. It was a prison officer on 'C' wing. "Joy, can you come over to see Darren H. He has returned from visits with some bad news. We are not sure what it is but could you see him. We haven't started serving tea yet so perhaps you could see him before then."

There was nothing else for it but to go. Hopefully after a chat with Darren, his situation might not seem so bad. I left the office at a quick pace, hoping to get home at a reasonable time if I was lucky. Moving through 'B' wing, I heard my name being called. Senior Officer Pike was trying to attract my attention. The wing was busy with men going to the servery area to collect their tea. I headed back to the confines of the wing office, where it was somewhat quieter and we could speak in private. "I've left a message on the chaplaincy phone but now I've seen you, all the better," he said. "It's John S. He's just returned from visits and it sounds as though this will be his girl's last. We are concerned because, as you know, he's on a self-harm watch. We shall be locking up shortly for tea. Perhaps you could come when we open up for evening association." There was no other chaplain on duty so it was down to me to offer what support

I could. That's the nature of the job. I'd rather go home with a clear conscience knowing I had responded to a cry for help.

My time with Darren was relatively short. He had managed to make one or two phone calls home courtesy of the wing officer, and that put his mind at ease. After a conversation with me, he was able to see the way ahead much more clearly. I assured him of the chaplaincy team's support and left him to have tea. Problems for the prisoner are heightened because he's often at the mercy of restrictions in prison that he wouldn't encounter in the community. If we can help alleviate this, it's to everyone's benefit, not least of all, the prisoner and his family.

I returned to the office and made a call home. This wasn't the first time I had been late and Eric was used to unforeseen circumstances calling for my attention, whether in prison or church. The good news was it was a nice, sunny evening and the drive home would be pleasant. I looked at the clock. I would be at least another 45 minutes before 'B' wing opened and I could see John.

By the time I arrived on the wing, most cell doors were open and men were busy making phone calls or queuing waiting their turn. Some were playing pool and others were making the most of the short time they had out on association. I located John and we found space to talk in private, courtesy of the senior officer in his office. It was sometimes difficult to see how one can make a difference in the lives of men with such complex issues. However, if I really thought that, then there would be little point in me being there and I knew with certainty this was the place were God had called me to minister.

I knew John and something about his background. In some ways it was easier to get a handle on his situation. Whoever you are, it's never a pleasant feeling to know your loved one has called time on your relationship. Being in prison, the effect is felt more keenly because of the limitations of your restricted surroundings. After all, it's not an option to put your coat on and go out for a walk when you feel like it!

John talked and I listened. I did a lot of that over the next half hour or so. I was hopeful that once locked up again, he would at least get through the night and tomorrow we could pick up again. He had a supportive pad mate, the name given to cell mates. I gave what I considered to be helpful insights into his situation and left John, having a brief conversation with the officer and making notes before leaving for home.

I was able to enjoy the scenic route home over the Lincolnshire Wolds. What did it matter if I was later than usual? At least I was able leave the prison—unlike those I left behind. Tomorrow was another day, bringing its own set of joys and heartache. I prayed John would reach it in relative peace.

1. 'Turn, Turn, Turn.' by The Byrd's.
   Columbia Records 1965

Chapter Nine
Cell No. Six

By the time I returned to work the following morning, John from 'B' wing had gone to meet with his solicitor in the visits room, which was inside the prison estate but outside the main prison wings. I hoped to catch up with him later, depending on what time he returned to the wing. In the meantime, I took my share of the statutory duties and visited the men in the segregation block. There were six in today. Not bad for a Friday but all could change in a moment.

It was a while since I had visited and it was good to catch up with staff too, showing friendship and support, and an interest in their lives. After all, the chaplain was for the whole prison, staff and prisoners alike. I didn't mind being teased because I was a Yellowbelly, the name for Lincolnshire natives, or a Cod Head, the nickname for people from Grimsby, which was once the largest fishing port in the country. I was also ribbed that the Mariners, Grimsby Town FC, didn't match up to The Imps, Lincoln City FC. It was all good banter with the prison officers.

It started off as a fairly straightforward round of visits, with one of the on-duty officers opening up the cell door of each man. If I hadn't met the inmate before, there would be an introduction along the lines of "Hello, my name is Joy, chaplain on duty today. How are you? Is there anything I can help you with?"

Even though I had a clerical (dog) collar on, it was not always apparent that I was from the church. Sometimes inmates were alarmed, thinking I was the bearer of bad news. Mostly it was a help. The chaplain could often speak up, be supportive and intervene in a situation where other staff couldn't. We were used to pushing the boundaries if necessary.

We arrived at the sixth cell. There was a pause before the door was opened. The officer accompanying me turned and said: "You need to be aware that this man is only having liquids." "Oh", I replied, "is he on a hunger strike?" I was surprised I hadn't heard about this. "No", came the answer, "I think it's a religious fast."

This was even more unusual as the prisoner wasn't a Muslim and anyway it wasn't Ramadan or any major fast days of other faiths. I was intrigued to know more.

"Has he been making any demands or asking for a move to another prison?" I asked. "No, he just seems content to read or sit and pray when not out on exercise, although he is due for a move soon to be nearer court hearings—but that's been on the cards for some time."

The door opened to reveal a shaft of light streaming through the narrow window that overlooked the exercise yard. For a moment, it blinded me and then suddenly, before my eyes, the prisoner appeared and held out his hand. "Hello, I'm Terry." Because I'd been briefed about his restricted diet, I expected to find a pasty, thin, depressed looking individual. Instead, he was bright-eyed, sharp and keen to engage in conversation. What struck me was his face, which had a distinct glow and appeared to be as bright as the sun lighting up the cell. I stepped inside, glancing at my accompanying officer for a nod of confirmation. He kept a discreet distance but near enough to intervene if need be. I thought it unlikely that there would be any bother but I was best to be guided by the officer.

Turning to Terry, I enquired: "Tell me about yourself; why are you not eating?"

"Well," he replied, "although I am registered Church of England, I don't attend Sunday chapel services. I have my reasons for not going."

I understood to a certain extent. There were probably other prisoners he didn't want to come in contact with and felt safer staying away. As he was moving soon, it seemed irrelevant to pursue this part of the conversation.

"I was brought up to attend chapel," he continued. "In fact, my dad was a lay preacher for many years. I do have faith in God. I expect you find that hard to believe, with me being in prison."

I didn't think he was expecting an answer to that statement. The quote from the Danish philosopher and theologian, Soren Kierkegaard came to mind: "God creates out of nothing. Wonderful you say. Yes, to be sure but He does, what is still more wonderful: He makes saints out of sinners."[1]

I wasn't here to judge Terry or the reason he was here. I'd seen and heard of many conversion experiences in prison to know that people can change, lead good and honest lives and go on to serve God, even becoming ministers and clergy.

Who knows, Terry might even follow in his father's footsteps and become a preacher.

"I don't mind being in the seg," he said. "It has given me time and space for thinking, reflecting on the past with all its mistakes, and considering my future. I've got my Gideon's bible and a few other Christian books and leaflets I've collected over time which I've been reading. I know some folk won't believe I can change but I'm determined to get right with God and make something of my life and for my parents to be proud of me. My probation officer is very supportive and my solicitor thinks I may get a suspended sentence, or at least be released early, considering the time I have already done. Whatever happens, my family are behind me and systems are being put into place for my support."

His words certainly sounded convincing. He didn't have to prove anything to me: it was between him and God. But it was heartening to think I could be a small part of his movement towards rehabilitation and a good future. It didn't seem as though our conversation was going much further, so I offered to pray with him. Before I could get the words out of my mouth, Terry said: "It's possible I may not see you again before I go and I know a Christian minister may not be on duty over the weekend, so would you bring me communion please?"

I had to agree with him. In the life of the prison, it's best to seize the moment and plan for today. "Yes, I will be pleased to bring communion to you," I replied. "I'm hopeful that I may get back before dinner time."

Terry was immensely grateful but I went away, knowing that it was going to be a tight squeeze, as Friday was early dinner due to Muslim Friday prayers. I was fortunate to have, on duty with me that morning, a Methodist lay-chaplain who was willing to assist if necessary. Before leaving the seg, I recorded in the daily journal information about the prisoners I had seen and spoke to the senior officer about my proposed return with communion before dinner. He was most obliging and keen for this to happen.

"We'll be ready for you," he called after me as I went on my way, unlocking and locking doors securely behind me. As soon as I stepped outside the seg, who should be walking past but my colleague Michael. How fortunate to have bumped into him. God certainly works in mysterious ways!

I explained about the situation with Terry. Michael was pleased to be invited to assist me with administering communion. We talked over our work schedule so far. "I'll meet you back here in 45 minutes with the communion elements and all we need for the short service to take place," I said. "Please don't be late or else we will run over into dinnertime."

Michael continued on his journey to 'B' wing and I went in the opposite direction, bypassing the chaplaincy office en-route to the chapel. I entered via the top stairs and made my way down to the cupboard containing the resources for chapel services. Rarely did I need to access the cupboard; until this point, the Anglican chaplain normally took charge of weekend chapel services and individual communion. All this was going to change, as I was to discover over the next few months. At this moment though, it was down to me to gather together the wine, wafers, books and bible for Holy Communion. I scoured the cupboard for the portable communion set but couldn't find it. Never mind, there was no point in wasting time in looking further.

I took the chalice, bottle of wine, wafers, silver tray, wooden cross and cloths, locked the cupboard door and picked up the order of service for communion together with a bible. I grabbed a carrier from the kitchen, put everything in it and went on my way. Passing by the chaplaincy office, I left a note on the desk for anyone wondering where I was.

I got back to the seg with ten minutes to spare and waited for Michael. He wasn't long; I heard keys rattling in the doors and Michael appeared, ready for what lay ahead.

Senior Officer Jackson appeared. "I've got a bottle of communion wine in this bag," I said to him. He looked at me, eyebrows raised. "When you've got what you want out, I'd better take charge of it. We don't want it falling into the wrong hands, do we?" A slight smile appeared on his face. I knew exactly what he meant!

The three of us walked to cell number six. The door opened and Michael and I entered. Terry had moved a small cardboard table and chair to the centre of the room. Apart from these two items, the only other furnishings in the cell were the toilet, sink and a low bed. Another prison officer appeared at the door with two chairs for us. I was grateful for his thoughtfulness. It was good to have the option to sit if needed.

I began removing communion items from the bag I brought and laid the white cloth on the table. I reflected on my own church with its Wesleyan Evangelical tradition. I recalled the many Anglican churches, cathedrals and abbeys I had visited, with their beautiful stained-glass windows, artefacts, carvings and historical features. I thought of the beautiful icons and church furnishings I had seen in Our Lady RC Church in Lincoln. And yet here, in this sparse cell, God was also present and there was a sense that we were standing on Holy ground. I poured a small amount of wine into the chalice, knowing I would drink any wine that remained. I handed the bottle to the officer, after which he left the cell with the door ajar and the lock thrown so we wouldn't be inadvertently locked in. When the table was ready, I handed to Terry and Michael the order of service and read from the bible, the account of the last supper from Luke's gospel.

From where I stood, I could just catch sight of an officer sitting discreetly outside the cell. The sun had moved slightly and skimmed the side of Terry's head, lighting up his already blond hair. Its rays came to rest on some photographs stuck on the wall above his bed. Perhaps they were of his family. Terry had already spoken about his father. We proceeded with the service and shared the bread and wine together. I concluded with a prayer and asked Terry if he would like me to pray with him. He didn't hesitate in saying yes.

There as a knock on the door. Senior Officer Jackson appeared and said: "Dinner will be coming down in ten minutes. When you've eaten it, pack up your belongings ready for moving to reception at 1.30 p.m. Then it's on your way to the next prison."

We looked at him in amazement. Moves were often done earlier in the morning. However, I'd been in the service long enough to know that things sometimes happen outside the norm, that there's always a reason for it and that we don't need to know what the reason is. Even if we asked, we would be unlikely to get an answer that satisfied us.

"Michael, would you clear the table?" I asked, "and don't forget to pick up the wine from the Senior Officer. I'll have a conversation with Terry before he leaves the prison."

"Well Terry," I continued. "This is a surprise, isn't it? You're moving today."

He looked at me intently. This was prison and we both knew it was not like catching a train when, for the most part, you could rely on the train arriving. The phrase seize the moment had taken on a new meaning this morning. It would be fair to say that God's hand had been at work to bring about this Holy meeting. Terry still had that glow on his face, which so struck me when we first saw met.

"Are you apprehensive about moving?" I asked, thinking he could be getting nervous. "Oh no," he replied, "it's one more step along the way to getting my life back on track again."

The words of the hymn by Sydney Carter came to mind:
"One more step along the world I go,
One more step along the world I go,
From the old things to the new,
Keep me travelling along with you;
As I travel through the bad and good,
Keep me travelling the way I should;
Where I see no way to go,
You`ll be telling me the way, I know.
And it's from the old I travel to the new;
Keep me travelling along with you."[2]

We shared more conversation and prayers and I left him to prepare for the next journey, confident in the fact that God was with him at all times and in all places.

1. The Journals of Soren Kierkgaard b 1838 Translations include `A selection from the journals of S.K. 1938 by Alexander Dru. Papers and journals 1966 by Alistair Hannay
2. 'One more step along the world I go' by Sydney Carter 1971 Stainer and Bell Ltd Admin.
   Hope Publissshing Co. Hymnary.org

Chapter Ten
Stay Close to the Cracks

Stay close to the cracks
To the broken places
Where people weep and cry out in pain.
Stay close to the cracks
Where God's tears fall
And God's wounds bleed
For love of us.
Stay close to the cracks
Where the light shines in
And grass pushes up
Through concrete
Stay close to the cracks
Where wounds
Open doorways
To healing and wholeness and life.
Christine Sine.

This reflection was written in response to Leonard Cohen's song 'Anthem' [1], which reminds us there indeed is a crack in everything but this is not a reason for despair, but rather hope for this is how the light gets in.

In his book, 'Eager to Love', Richard Rohr[2] comments that St Francis of Assisi asks us to stay close to the cracks in the social fabric of our world. It's a thought worth reflecting on. Everything in our lives and our world has cracks, wounds and broken places that tell of pain and suffering. Sometimes we try to cover them over but this only makes them fester and get worse. Yet it is in the cracks—the broken places of our lives where violence flares and pain cries out—that healing also happens. When we acknowledge imperfections and the pain they cause, we take the first step towards wholeness.

I think of the many reasons men and women find themselves in prison. I have listened to their stories. Of course, I realise I only hear one side of the story, which may or may not be true. However, I am not there to judge, only listen and, if requested, offer advice and prayer. Many times on the wing, unable to have the cell door unlocked, I have conducted a conversation with the prisoner through the crack and hinges at the side of the door. Not the ideal situation but better than nothing. I came to discover that in prison, there are many ways and means of carrying out your ministry that is not applicable to parish life. The freedom we take for granted in the community is not available in prison and one has to adapt and make use of the resources—or lack of them— and carry on in the hope of a positive outcome, or at least a move forward that will enable the prisoner to see a light at the end of the tunnel.

The light was often discovered in chapel services.

"How do you feel about taking a service on a Saturday once a month for 'E' wing?" asked the co-coordinating chaplain.

There were two weekend services: one on Sunday for the main wings and the other on Saturday for the more vulnerable prisoners. They couldn't share worship together for various reasons. I was looking forward to this additional ministry with the men. No doubt it would have its challenges, but my contact so far with 'E' wing had been positive. Generally speaking, I found the men to be courteous and receptive to the chaplaincy team.

My allotted slot was two weeks away, which seemed a long time. In essence, it wasn't. Fortunately I had a pianist and the local prison fellowship group to offer their support, which they did wholeheartedly. It was down to me to arrange the order of service and co-ordinate the group's participation in the service. That was all well and good but what about me, and what was I going to say that would strike a chord with the men?

My thoughts went back to my training at theological college. A full-blown theological sermon would not fit the bill here. I pondered on this and then a thought crossed my mind. No, I couldn't possibly... could I?

I reflected on a children's address that I had given one time at my church, called 'The Doughnut with a Hole'. The basis of this is when life gets tough and the going hard; concentrate on the doughnut and not the hole. I liked this illustration, which can apply to anyone of us, whether we like doughnuts or not.

Yes, there was a lot I could do with this illustration. There were some in prison who could not read or write but they could listen and look. Hopefully this illustration would be an aid to shine some light on the Christian message. The service was arranged, Saturday came and I arrived at the prison gate with my bag containing the bible, books and 36 doughnuts!

"Good morning, Joy," said Ron, the gateman on duty, "Is it 'E' wing service today?" "Yes," I replied. "I've got four volunteers and a pianist arriving shortly, plus six packets of doughnuts in my bag." "Oh, you're having a change from biscuits then," Ron replied. "Yes," I said, "something like that!" I didn't enlighten him further. He would probably hear about the doughnuts anyway.

I was busy getting the chapel ready for the service, lighting altar candles, sorting hymn books, preparing lectionary readings and arranging chairs. The sound of voices echoed up the back stairs as I got the mugs, tea and coffee ready in the kitchen. The local prison fellowship group was so supportive and faithfully came to the services on a regular basis.

"What's this Joy, doughnuts? We are having a treat today," said Stephen. "Yes, they're here for a sermon illustration," I replied, "as well as to eat afterwards." He looked puzzled and although he didn't say so, I think he thought I had lost the plot!

The men arrived for the service. At least they were on time, which didn't always happen. There were 24 due, which was a good number. However, 25 arrived. Still, there would be enough doughnuts for those who wanted them.

The service got underway. We sang hymns, read the scriptures and prayed until the time came for me to give the sermon. We were on a tight time schedule compared with church services: one hour maximum to include refreshments and fellowship afterwards.

I stood up. Carefully lifting the doughnut to eye level, I announced: "I've brought something with me this morning. I expect you know what it is." Everyone looked at me but no one spoke. Not quite the response I expected. I was standing a distance away from the men so moving forward, I said: "Now can you see what it is?" thinking maybe they had not seen one for a long time.

They gazed intently at the doughnut for a few seconds until one of the men piped up: "Is it a doughnut, miss?" "Yes," I replied, glad that at last we were getting somewhere. So were the rest of the men who broke into a rapture of cheering and clapping. Again, not quite the response I was expecting but at least I had their attention.

"What else do you see?" More silence. Then came the next answer.

"You can see through it."

"Why's that then?" I asked.

"There's a hole where the doughnut should be."

They had more or less given the right answers so I pressed on while also noticing that I had got the attention of the two officers who were on duty at the back of the chapel. They smiled. The sermon was for all of us, after all. Everyone one of us can get stuck in a hole at various times in our lives and often can't see the wood for the trees.

I pressed on with the remainder of the sermon, reminding them that for the Christian, keeping our eyes upon Jesus will aid us to live a life that's honest and good. Try to focus on what's wholesome and true. To look at a hole only, we see nothing before us—only emptiness and dark.

The men listened and seem to grasp what I was saying but I also suspect that they had their eyes on the plates of doughnuts.

The final hymn was sung and the benediction pronounced. The men lost no time in making their way for coffee. I got there before them.

"Who would like a doughnut?" I asked.

"Nice one miss!" someone shouted. Another cheer went up. I made sure all got one who wanted one.

"Aren't you eating yours, Dave?" I asked, looking over at a slim young man chatting to one of the volunteers. "No, I'm taking it back to my pad to eat at dinner."

"I will put it in a serviette for you; otherwise you'll have sugar and grease all over you."

"Do you know, miss, I've never eaten a doughnut for years."

"Well as long as you remember what the symbol of the hole means."

"Oh, I will, I will," came the reply. "Will you be taking our service again?"

"Yes," I replied, "but don't expect doughnuts every time!"

It was a good start to my Saturday services and I was looking forward to the next one. But as I was soon to discover, it was going to be very different from this one.

1. Leonard Cohen 'The essential Leonard Cohen' 1992 Sony BMG Music Entertainment
2. Eager to Love by Richard Rohr. Hodder and Stoughton 2015

Chapter Eleven
The Yellow Rose

Wednesday morning began on a smooth note. Most of the chaplains on duty managed to meet for morning prayers before the busy day began. Always a good start!

Unusually, there were only six men to be seen on induction and three in the block. All were English, so there was no need of the language interpreter facility. The rest of the morning continued in an equally straightforward fashion. Dinnertime arrived and the chaplains took their places on the various wings at the meal queues. Many prisoners took the opportunity of having a quick word with the chaplain during these times. The officers also had a chance for conversation with the chaplain while keeping a watchful eye on the servery area. Usually, one of the trusted prisoners had charge of the menu selections, so there could be no disputing who had ordered what. The queues grew smaller and men were busy taking meals back to their cells to be eaten alone or in the presence of a pad mate.

Then the atmosphere suddenly changed. Radios bleeped. There was a flurry of activity. Prison officers sped down the wings. Staff and inmates jumped out of the way. We knew something had happened.

The chaplaincy office was deserted. Perhaps my colleagues had decided to take their lunch break while they could. I settled down to eat my sandwiches and had just begun to enjoy a quiet moment when the coordinating chaplain appeared at the door. I could sense something was the matter – and that it was serious. Before I could speak, he piped up: "I've just come from 'C' wing. The police and ambulance were there but it was too late."

Death in Custody is the term used for a suicide.

"Who was it?" I asked, as if knowing was going to make it alright.

"Gerry S," came the reply. I turned away, not wanting him to see the tears in my eyes. I recalled the many conversations we had had over the time Gerry had been in prison. What had brought him to this point? I felt sick to my stomach. There would be an enquiry and an inquest, and what about his family? The Prison Service family liaison officer would be an important link here, assisted by the chaplain if necessary.

Lunch finished and the afternoon's activities commenced. An air of despondency hovered over the landings in 'C' wing. The chaplaincy team supported prisoners and staff alike, bringing some relief to a delicate situation. Gerry was well liked and seemed to get on with everyone. I knew his case was coming up shortly and wondered if this had played on his mind. He hadn't been in prison before and found the experience a difficult one. Regular contact with prison officers, nurses and staff from other agencies had not prevented his tragic death. In the following days and weeks, the chaplaincy team continued to support vulnerable prisoners and especially those placed on special watch.

It was some weeks later that the coordinating chaplain approached me and said: "The lads on 'C' wing have asked if they can have a memorial service for Gerry. I thought that you might like to take charge as you have had a lot of contact with him." I felt honoured to have been asked and said yes straight away, although I wasn't sure how this would work out as, clearly, the whole wing couldn't attend.

The date was set and notices displayed for applications to attend the service. As it happened, 40 men put their names forward and, on the day, 35 came. I was pleased to see so many wanting to pay their respects to Gerry.

The memorial service was part of the normal weekend service and included Holy Communion. Three Prison Fellowship volunteers attended. The duty governor for the day also came, which I thought was a nice gesture. I prepared a short responsive service sheet for us to use, remembering Gerry and his life. I also brought in 40 yellow roses, which the gate officers commented on. When I said what they were going to be used for, I got a very sensitive response.

The chapel was prepared; introductory music was played by the pianist and the orderly group of prisoners arrived. For some, it was their first time at in chapel. As I was handing out the order of service, I was also aware that some men couldn't read. But better to feel part of the group and for all to have a sheet, and anyway, it was a memento of the service. There was a sense of expectancy as I explained to the attentive group just how the service was going to proceed. Considering some were unfamiliar with it, they were well behaved and listened intently. The 40 yellow roses lay on a table nearby, ready to be laid on or near the altar. Small candles on a stand would be lit in remembrance of Gerry and also to reflect Jesus as the Light of the world.

The service proceeded with prayers, readings and hymns. I read from the bible, gave a short homily and spoke about Gerry, reflecting on his life and what I knew of him. I intended to invite others to share their thoughts if they wished but before I could speak, a blond-haired lad sitting in the front row piped up: "Can I say something, Miss?" "Yes," I replied and with that, he was on his feet.

"He was a good bloke," the lad continued. "He always looked out for me and I know he had a good family who visited him. I shall miss him." Sitting down, he sniffed and rubbed his left sleeve across his eyes to catch falling tears. His comments were the catalyst for others to speak and they weren't shy in rising from their seats to do so. Many echoed that Gerry was a "decent, dependable bloke". One might wonder how he had come to be in prison, but this service of remembrance wasn't dependent on this fact. Gerry was a human being made in the image of God and had somehow gone astray.

I felt the same sadness as these lads and reflected on some words by John Donne:

"No man is man island…any man's death diminishes me, because I am involved in mankind". [1]

We came to the part of the service where I invited inmates to lay a rose at the altar and to light a candle, if they wished. Everyone did. It was a humbling few minutes as I led the way, followed by the duty governor. Soon the altar was strewn with a sea of yellow roses. Some were placed on the platform carpet and others around the sides of the altar. Candles were lit on the stand adjacent to the lectern. As the flowers were being laid, many men did the sign of the cross and some knelt before the altar. It was a remarkable and humbling sight, and one that has always remained with me. These men were not able to go to Gerry's funeral but participated in an act of remembrance that meant an awful lot to them.

We concluded with prayers, and the men were most appreciative of the service. Over coffee and biscuits, they expressed thanks and gratitude. Eventually the time came for them to make their way back to their cells. The volunteers left the prison and I remained in the chapel. An air of silence fell, interrupted only by the occasional shout and noise of prison life.

I reflected on the service and thought about Gerry's family and friends. How were they coping? Change comes when someone close dies. Life is never the same again. It was apparent that through the depth of feeling shown at the service, there would be men on 'C' wing needing extra support. I surveyed the roses scattered around the chapel. It seemed a shame to move them but if I didn't put them in vases, they would soon perish. I just about found enough vases in the chapel kitchen cupboard for them all. They looked an impressive sight and would lift the spirits of all who entered. Of that I was sure.

Thinking about the lads, I decided to take a vase to the wing at lunchtime. I put the flowers in a sturdy bag, to avoid any mishaps along the way. My arrival was met with warm greetings. Lock-up began and I took my place by a small table, which was home to the large salt pot and vinegar container and adjacent to the servery area. I placed the filled vase on the table. From there, it would reside in the Senior Officer's office.

Lunch was about to be served. A loud call echoed around the wings. 'C' Four! The top landing cells were opened and down came the men to the meal queue. It suddenly got very noisy as the men chatted away to one another. Gradually, they made their way over to my table and it wasn't long before the vase was spotted.

"Are they the roses from the chapel?" a tall, dark-haired lad asked. "Yes," I replied, "I thought you would like to see them again. I'm going to put them in the office when dinner has finished."

"I've never been to chapel before," he said. "I didn't know what to expect but I'm glad I went. Gerry would have been well chuffed to know we all were there remembering him".

"Yes", I echoed, "I think he would."

Senior Officer Brown was entering his office as I placed the vase on the desk next to the phone. "Well, I've never been brought roses before," he quipped. I explained their part in the service. "I heard about it," he said, "The men were full of talk about what happened. I think you made a good impression on them, Joy". "Well, I was just doing my job," I replied.

In the life of the prison, we never know what a day may hold or what situations will be faced. For the prison chaplain, faith, hope and courage are an integral part of their make-up. As I pondered on the service and how we had committed ourselves into God's keeping, I reflected on the words from the prophet Micah:

"And what does the Lord require of you but to do justice, and to love kindness, and to walk humbly with your God" (Micah 6:8) (RSV).

1. No Man is an Island by John Donne, Devotions upon Emergent Occasions, mediation 17 1624.

Chapter Twelve
Team Work

On arrival at the prison on Monday morning, the first person I saw on entering the gate was Senior Officer Brown, who was on duty during Saturday's memorial service for Gerry.

"How are the yellow roses doing?" I asked, half expecting to hear they had perished or been moved somewhere else. "They have blossomed out a treat," he answered. "In fact, we have split the bunch and taken some to the other wing office. I had a water bottle in my rucksack so drank the remains and refuelled with more water and added some roses. Job done. Very nice!" "What a kind gesture", I replied. "It cheers up others for the day, doesn't it?" He said, and went on his way.

My thoughts went back to the death of the late Princess Diana. The public laid flowers outside the railings at Buckingham Palace; not just a few bunches—small piles became almost mountains. Folk came from far and near and even travelled from overseas to pay their respects to a remarkable and much-loved princess. Flowers were strewn everywhere, such was the depth of feeling for the People's Princess, and it didn`t stop there. On the funeral day, as the cortege made its way slowly out of London to the princess's final resting place at Althorp House, in Northampton, flowers were thrown onto the hearse carrying the coffin. People lined the roads for miles, all throwing flowers. Such was the depth of emotion felt by so many.

There is a sentiment that echoes the giving and receiving of flowers: say it with flowers. Flowers give us an opportunity to say something, although not necessarily with words. The lads on 'C' wing were able to say it with flowers. The yellow rose denotes kindness, friendship and caring.

Listening to the comments made by Gerry's prison associates, he certainly had these attributes. I was pleased to hear such comments from Senior Officer Brown but having known him for a number of years, I didn't expect anything less!

I arrived at the chaplaincy office with time to catch up on my emails. One caught my immediate attention. It was from Senior Officer Sheldon asking if I could arrange a chaplaincy training package on the POELT (Prison Officer Entry Level Training) session next Tuesday. This was something I enjoyed doing, meeting with prospective prison officers on their training programme and giving a presentation of the role of chaplains within the prison service.

The new trainees were usually a mix of male and female of various age groups. It was a relaxed session with time for questions, of which there were usually a few.

I spoke briefly of how I came to be working in the prison and how it was not only a job but my vocation and Christian calling. I found it useful, and hopefully for the class sitting before me, to speak on a personal level. Theirs would be a very different role to mine. I had nothing but respect and admiration for prison officers as they were instructed in their future work within a team which would be demanding, physically and emotionally. There were many aspects to their jobs, not least of all to be key workers, mentors and guides to prisoners in their charge.

The chaplaincy was just one department in the prison service that these new recruits would see. Included were probation, education, resettlement and others.

It was good to have some working time away from the business of the prison.

During the early years of working in the prison, I had my church ordination service as an ordained elder. This was a special occasion for me, my family, church, chaplain colleagues and all who had supported me through the years of ministerial training. It hadn't gone unnoticed by my two training officer colleagues. I was very touched to receive a white bible from them with the inscription: "Congratulations upon your appointment into the church. You have been described as a breath of fresh air within the walls of the prison by a P.O.E.L.T." We often don't know how someone else sees us. For the chaplain to retain a faithful vision in a difficult environment is of paramount importance.

It had been a busy morning in the prison and I was pleased when lunchtime arrived. I decided to have a break and went across the road to Lincoln County Hospital where they had an excellent self-service restaurant. Over the years, I got to know some of the staff, so it was always good to catch up with them and have a brief chat. I managed to get a window seat in the restaurant and enjoyed my lunch looking out over the Lincolnshire countryside. How fortunate, I thought to myself, as I gazed at the landscape outside, unlike the prisoners in cells eating their lunch. Theirs would be a very restricted view between bars on the window. For some, they may get a glimpse of the top of Lincoln Cathedral; for others, it would be the exercise yards where they spent part of each day.

I cleared my pots and made my way back to the prison. On exiting the lift, I turned right and started to walk along the corridor. Coming my way was a prison officer called Rob. He was a big burly man, dependable, very kind and someone who I would call the salt of the earth.

"Hello," I said, "have we got someone in hospital?" thinking he was coming to relieve another officer in charge of a prisoner. "I've come to visit my mother, who was brought in yesterday. She is in very frail health and at 86 it's not looking good. Have you got time to say hello to her?"

"Of course," I said and followed him into a ward of mostly elderly patients. In front of us, lay a delicate, sickly looking lady. Her grey hair had been brushed back and she eyed us both with a steely stare.

"How are you, Mam?" Rob's voice seemed to surprise her.

Not waiting for an answer he went on: "I've brought the prison chaplain to visit you, her name is Joy". Her eyes seemed to light up as I bent down, clasped her hand and asked:' "Tell me your name." The reply was slow in coming but she said: "Elsie." "And how are you today, Elsie?" I enquired. She couldn't manage to tell me. I glanced at Rob. It was hard for him. Of course, patients of any age can rally. We could hope and pray that whatever the outcome, Elsie would be as comfortable and peaceful as possible. I assured them both I would visit again and headed back to the prison.

I was scheduled to attend a self-harm review and it was important that I be there. A wing was adjacent to the chaplain's office so I arrived at the 2:30 pm meeting in good time. Someone from probation was already there. The rest of the team making up the review board would arrive shortly. We made ourselves comfortable in Senior Officer Butler's office and took the opportunity of caching up on prison news. I always enjoyed a close relationship with colleagues from other departments and it was good to get to know more of the value of their work and how it fitted into the life of the prisoner.

Soon the inmate arrived. Having been in the prison for three weeks, Danny was now starting to look more relaxed. The support and care that he was receiving was clearly having an effect. SO Butler conducted the review with sensitivity and all present agreed the level of observation for Danny could now be reduced, but he would still have continuing care from all departments. I was particularly pleased he had started to attend chapel services on Sundays. At least he was feeling confident mixing with other prisoners and also, the chaplain and volunteers would have a chance for more conversation with him. Things were looking much brighter all round.

The clock soon moved round to teatime and I prepared for home. Stepping through the gate, I glanced across at the hospital and wondered how Elsie's afternoon had been.

It was February and fortunately winter had so far managed to be relatively snow free, at least in Lincolnshire. Mornings were cold, sometimes frosty and icy. This particular morning didn't seem too bad as I headed off out of town towards the main road to Lincoln. It was already getting light and in the distance the sun peeped through. I wasn't the only member of staff to travel a long distance to work and there were several officers who lived in my area.

One was Nev Horton, who was a great conversationalist and as he mainly worked on 'B' wing, which was near the chaplain's office; we often saw him en-route to another part of the prison. Rarely did we get through the wing without stopping to talk. And it was a pleasure to do so! He was such a pleasant guy, and he supported Grimsby Town FC so all the more reason to chat!

The temperature had gone up today and the roads seemed free of ice. Strangely enough, there didn't seem to be an awful lot of traffic and I was able to travel at a reasonable speed. This I was doing, until I caught sight of a blue police accident sign.

Beyond this, was a yellow traffic diversion sign. Oh dear, this was bad news for someone. I pressed on and eventually re-joined the main road. Traffic was flowing freely and there was no sight of any accident.

I arrived at the prison not much later than usual. The other chaplains on duty had already made a start on some of the duties for the day. It was left for me to visit the healthcare wing. I discovered there were ten men to see. Most of them I knew already and hopefully they were doing well and could soon be moved onto the main wings. I touched base with the staff on duty and made a start on my rounds.

Jamie was a young man on remand and this was his first time in prison. On the face of It, he was a personable guy, however, the nature of his alleged crime would leave him vulnerable and open to possible attack from other prisoners, hence, his stay in healthcare for the moment. We had been chatting for several minutes when I caught sight of the duty governor outside the cell door. She didn't seem to be moving in any particular direction. Eventually, there was a knock on the door. She poked her head in and asked to speak with me. The governor was a busy person and would not be waiting around unless it was important. I concluded my visit with Jamie and stepped outside to face the governor, who said: "Come into the office and take a seat." By this time I was getting rather concerned as to what could be the matter. She went on: "I know that you and other staff were later getting into work this morning due to the accident on the A46. I'm sorry to tell you that Nev Horton died at the scene. It's a terrible shock for all of us. He was a much-loved and respected prison officer and I know he had lots of time for chaplaincy. We will let the prison staff know of the funeral details as and when they become available."

She paused. "Are you alright?"

I stared at her and eventually said: "I don't know." I couldn't utter any more words. She rose to her feet, put her hand on my shoulder and said: "Take what time you need. I'll ask the staff to bring you a cup of tea."

Eventually, a nurse arrived with some tea. She was very kind and offered to stay with me. Like any death and especially one in sudden, tragic circumstances it would take time to process and work through. The grief we felt was only a part of what loved ones would be experiencing.

I drank my tea and leaving the office, found that most of the prisoners had gone out to the exercise yard. I told the staff that chaplaincy would return later and took refuge in the quietness of the chapel. I sat in front of the altar looking up at the cross, praying that Nev would be at peace. The tears rolled down my cheeks and I sobbed. There would be no more lively conversations on 'B' wing, accompanied by Nev's warm smile. I suddenly felt very tired and thought of the words of Jesus who said: "Come to me, all you who labour and are heavy laden, and I will give you rest" (Matt. 11; 28 (NKJV).

By the time I left the chapel, it was not far off lunch. Today I had brought some sandwiches with me, but getting some space and fresh air was more important. I worked within a supportive chaplaincy team and they were more than happy to hold the fort and take any telephone calls that should come over the lunch hour.

I headed over to the hospital and decided on a snack rather than a cooked meal. My thoughts turned to Elsie and although it was lunchtime, I felt sure that the nursing staff would not mind me paying her a brief visit, which would leave the afternoon free for her family. I set off for the ward and headed straight for the nursing station. As I approached, my eye caught sight of screens around a bed further along the ward. My request to the nurse to visit Elsie brought the response: "Are the family expecting you?"

"No," I replied, "but I have been supporting them." I was told to wait while she went to Elsie's bed, disappearing behind the screens. It was some minutes before she reappeared with Rob. His face was ashen and shoulders heavy. The nurse ushered us into a side room, closing the door softly behind her.

From his armchair, Rob stared down at the floor and said: "Mam died half an hour ago. The hospital rang to say she was failing fast. Thankfully most of the family arrived to be with her at the end. Would you conduct her funeral, Joy? Mam said what a nice lady you are, and Pat, my wife, and the rest of the family would be grateful."

The news of Elsie's death didn't come as a complete surprise but there's often a sense of disbelief that this can't really be happening, especially for the family. She was their mother, grandma and great grandma.

I assured Rob that I would conduct the funeral and felt humbled to have been invited to do so. We chatted for a while. I think Rob was grateful for the brief respite. Eventually he rose to leave, aware that he ought to return to his family and Elsie's bedside. I offered to join him and his family but he gently declined, saying he would invite me to his house in due course to discuss arrangements. I wondered if he had heard about Nev, but I didn't feel inclined to raise the matter.

At the hospital café, I found a quiet corner overlooking the car park. There were so many people coming and going, everyone with their own story to tell.

Back at the prison, sadness hung in the air. The news of Nev's death had shocked everyone. The chaplaincy team, care team and other support personnel were kept busy, offering support where needed.

The funeral was held at a quiet country parish church, near Nev's home. It was a tribute to Nev to see so many people attend his funeral, some travelling long distances to be there. Especially moving were the prison officers who formed a guard of honour for his coffin.

In contrast was the funeral I conduced for Rob's mother, Elsie, which was held in Lincoln. This dear lady had reached a great age. I spent a pleasant afternoon at Rob's home, who fed me a wealth of information regarding Elsie's life. She was one of seven children with one sister still living. My life seemed easy compared to hers, especially as she was left a widow in her 50s.

Rob and Pat led the family into the service. A few friends were already seated inside. Yes, it is sad to say goodbye to a loved one. The pain we feel reflects the depth of our love for them.

As I thought about Nev and Elsie, the words of Abraham Lincoln came to mind: "In the end, it's not the years in your life that count. It's the life in your years."

Chapter Thirteen
A Life Worth Living

There is one thing we can be sure of: that time never stands still. As a young girl, I had an autograph book in which someone had written the popular saying, 'time and tide wait for no man.' The seaside wasn't far from my home and I would often take the opportunity of standing on the promenade, watching the tide ebb and flow. Sometimes it would be a calm sea, at others, the sea would rage as the tide came in and high waves would crash into the sea wall. Life is a bit like that too. We can be living a life of relative calm and then a catastrophe happens, and our world seems to be crashing around us. People are merrily going about their everyday lives (or so it seems) and ours has ground to a halt. The way forward may be unsure and uncertain.

It's rather like that for the person who has found themselves in prison. Life has changed and the immediate future is unknown. The familiar has gone and a new pattern of daily life begins with a new set of people. Knowing who you can trust is not easy. For the most part, it is a case of survival and looking out for number one.

Personnel working with prisoners are there to help them in one way or another. Prison officers play a key role in not only keeping law and order, but assisting the men in their charge to make the most of their time in prison in purposeful activities. There can be opportunities for those who want to take advantage of what's on offer. Many who come into prison cannot read or write, so education classes can be a real help. In fact, many prisoners have gone on to earn degrees and learn a trade with qualifications in skills such as building and catering. Once the prisoner has settled down to life in prison, he can be directed to consider engaging in activities that will help him to adjust back into society and possible employment, when he's eventually released.

Prison can often be an opportunity to rekindle faith or to explore a chosen one. I was able to offer a variety of Christian courses, bible studies and worship services. A course that had tremendous impact and much success is the fifteen-week Alpha course[1], which has run successfully in churches over many years. I used it in my church and saw the effect it had had on people's lives. Folk felt comfortable in asking questions based on the DVD they had just watched. The course also includes a feedback questionnaire. One question in it is: "Would you have described yourself as a Christian at the beginning of the course?" Some of the answers are "not sure", "probably", "ish", and "yes, but without any real experience of a relationship with God". Group discussions gave an opportunity to ask questions in a relaxed environment. An experienced group leader would guide the group into discussing the topic which had just been viewed, although it was surprising what questions came up that seemed to be unrelated to the subject but clearly relevant to the person asking them.

There were occasions when the prisoner was unable to complete all the sessions. He may have other appointments that clashed with the course dates or moved on to another jail, or even released. However, nothing is wasted. It's possible he might be able to pick it up again at another jail or access the book Questions of Life, written by Nicky Gumbel, which the course is based on.

It was encouraging to see so many men grow in their faith and want to go deeper into their experience of knowing who Jesus Christ is, and how He fits into the pattern of salvation. Many men decided to accept Him as Saviour and some had a believer's baptism that took place during the weeks of the course, or in a chapel service.

A thank you card arrived on my desk in the chaplain's office from Carl. It said: "Just to say thank you for making my day so special when you baptised me on May 15th, and to everyone else involved. Many thanks. God Bless, Carl."

Another letter arrived by post from Jeffrey, who had moved to another jail nearing the end of the course. Part of what he wrote said: "I'm sorry I didn't get chance to say goodbye before I left Lincoln. I would like to thank you for the enlightenment I experienced on my spiritual path. It hasn't been an easy journey for me. For once, my life is so meaningful. I now walk through this life with a glow shining from within, full of peace, love, goodness, compassion and more. So once again, thank you for the time you have spent with me. It has been a life changing experience."

This is from Stuart: "I am now living with the Holy Spirit and am filled with joy and happiness. I wish I could have found the Lord under different circumstances. I regret what happened and am at peace with the Lord with His forgiveness."

Andrew, who moved to another jail, wrote: "I find silent times to pray and read my bible. This is giving me the strength to carry on. I seem to be reading the hymn 'What a Friend We Have in Jesus' as well. God's love be with you."

Ray, released just before Christmas, sent a festive card from himself and his wife: "Hello Joy, thank you for your support for me and fellow inmates while at Lincoln. I cannot tell you how much it was appreciated. May God help you to keep up the good work."

Carl wrote: "To everyone associated with Lincoln Prison Chaplaincy, especially Joy, Wendy and Steve who, in one way or another, have given me help in my times of need, as well as a caring ear in my times of hurt. I send this card filled with all my heart felt thank-you to you all."

Of course, the question remains: "Will faith be sustained on release from prison?" In some cases, we were able to make contact with a church in the area the prisoner was relocating to and which was willing to offer support to him. There are many organisations, churches and agencies which help and guide ex-offenders. Those with addictions and substance misuse issues can be directed to appropriate contacts. For the Christian, faith-based programmes at residential houses such as Betel, Teen Challenge, the Langley House Trust and others have a high success rate for integration back into society. The resettlement and probation teams work closely with those leaving prison.

There are many difficulties, hurdles and obstacles for the person leaving prison and with the right support there can be a positive outcome. Unfortunately there were occasions when the same faces returned to prison time after time. For some, it meant security and a roof over their heads. For others, old habits die hard. But the chaplains were always available to meet with all prisoners, regardless of circumstances.

Over the years that I worked in and around the prison, I walked many miles. As I conclude this book and reflect on the prisoners and their families I have met, from many diverse backgrounds and situations, I recall the words of an old American saying: "You can't understand someone until you've walked a mile in their shoes."

1. The Alpha Course is based on Alpha—Questions of life by Nicky Gumbel. Published by Alpha International. Holy Trinity Brompton 1993.